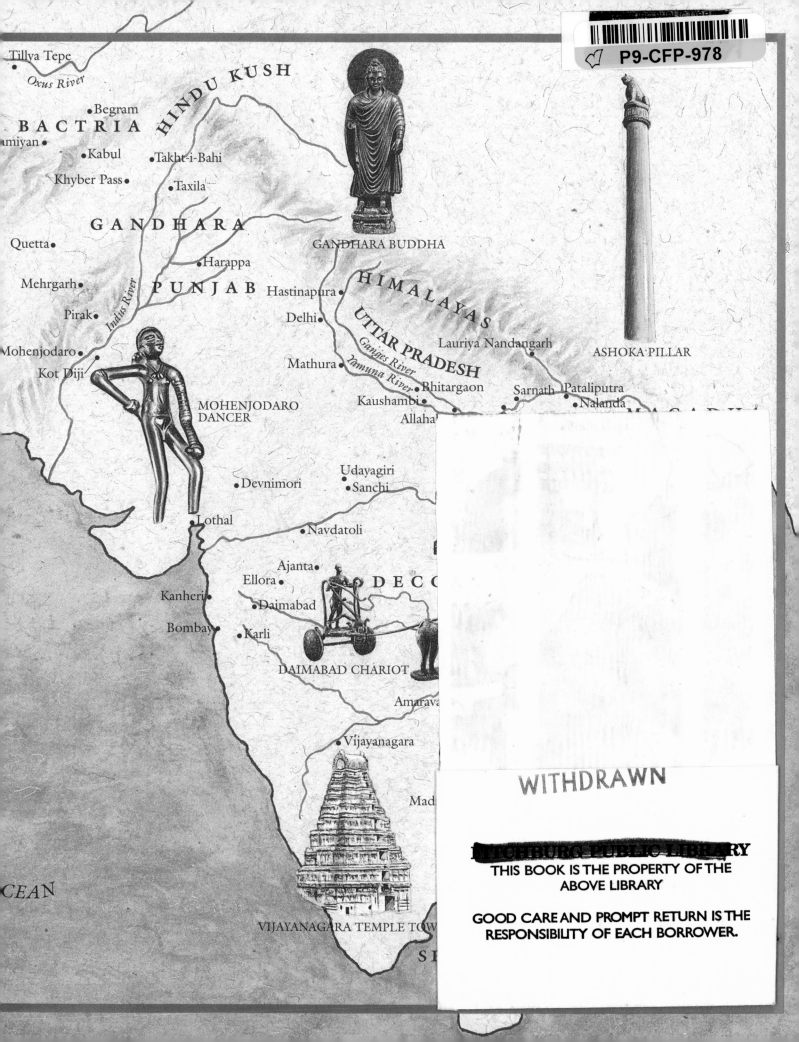

Tillya Tepe

Oxus River

HINDU KUSH

BACTRIA

Begram

amiyan

Kabul

Takht-i-Bahi

Khyber Pass

Taxila

GANDHARA

Quetta

GANDHARA BUDDHA

Harappa

Mehrgarh

PUNJAB

Hastinapura

HIMALAYAS

Pirak

Delhi

UTTAR PRADESH

Indus River

Ganges River

Lauriya Nandangarh

ASHOKA PILLAR

Mohenjodaro

Mathura

Yamuna River

Bhitargaon

Sarnath   Pataliputra

Kot Diji

Kaushambi

Nalanda

MOHENJODARO
DANCER

Allaha

Udayagiri

Devnimori

Sanchi

Lothal

Navdatoli

Ajanta

DECC

Ellora

Kanheri

Daimabad

Bombay

Karli

Amarava

DAIMABAD CHARIOT

Vijayanagara

Mad

CEAN

VIJAYANAGARA TEMPLE TOW

SI

Other Publications:

THE NEW HOME REPAIR AND
  IMPROVEMENT
JOURNEY THROUGH THE MIND
  AND BODY
WEIGHT WATCHERS® SMART CHOICE
  RECIPE COLLECTION
TRUE CRIME
THE AMERICAN INDIANS
THE ART OF WOODWORKING
ECHOES OF GLORY
THE NEW FACE OF WAR
HOW THINGS WORK
WINGS OF WAR
CREATIVE EVERYDAY COOKING
COLLECTOR'S LIBRARY OF THE
  UNKNOWN
CLASSICS OF WORLD WAR II
TIME-LIFE LIBRARY OF CURIOUS AND
  UNUSUAL FACTS
AMERICAN COUNTRY
VOYAGE THROUGH THE UNIVERSE
THE THIRD REICH
THE TIME-LIFE GARDENER'S GUIDE
MYSTERIES OF THE UNKNOWN
TIME FRAME
FIX IT YOURSELF
FITNESS, HEALTH & NUTRITION
SUCCESSFUL PARENTING
HEALTHY HOME COOKING
UNDERSTANDING COMPUTERS
LIBRARY OF NATIONS
THE ENCHANTED WORLD
THE KODAK LIBRARY OF CREATIVE
  PHOTOGRAPHY
GREAT MEALS IN MINUTES
THE CIVIL WAR
PLANET EARTH
COLLECTOR'S LIBRARY OF THE CIVIL
  WAR
THE EPIC OF FLIGHT
THE GOOD COOK
WORLD WAR II
THE OLD WEST

*For information on and a full description of
any of the Time-Life Books series listed above,
please call 1-800-621-7026 or write:*
Reader Information
Time-Life Customer Service
P.O. Box C-32068
Richmond, Virginia 23261-2068

Cover: A Harappan face and a Buddhist gateway testify to the great diversity of India's ancient cultural heritage. The 3,000-year-old carved steatite visage of the so-called Priest-King of Mohenjodaro seems to reflect a mood of tranquil meditation. Lion capitals and bas-reliefs with religious symbols and scenes from the life of Buddha adorn the southern gateway of the Great Stupa of Sanchi, considered by some to be the greatest Buddhist monument in India.

End paper: Painted by Paul Breeden on handmade Indian cotton paper with flecks of wool, this map shows the density and diversity of ancient India's cultures, some of which apparently traded with Mesopotamia and other distant lands. Breeden also painted the vignettes illustrating the timeline on pages 158-159.

ANCIENT INDIA: LAND OF MYSTERY

Time-Life Books is a division of TIME LIFE INC.

PRESIDENT and CEO: John M. Fahey Jr.

EDITOR-IN-CHIEF: John L. Papanek

TIME-LIFE BOOKS

MANAGING EDITOR: Roberta Conlan

Director of Design: Michael Hentges
Director of Editorial Operations: Ellen Robling
Director of Photography and Research: John Conrad Weiser
Senior Editors: Russell B. Adams Jr., Dale M. Brown, Janet Cave, Lee Hassig, Robert Somerville, Henry Woodhead
Special Projects Editor: Rita Thievon Mullin
Director of Technology: Eileen Bradley
Library: Louise D. Forstall

PRESIDENT: John D. Hall

Vice President, Director of Marketing: Nancy K. Jones
Vice President, New Product Development: Neil Kagan
Vice President, Book Production: Marjann Caldwell
Production Manager: Marlene Zack

Library of Congress Cataloging in Publication Data
Ancient India: land of mystery / by the editors of Time-Life Books.
    p. cm.—(Lost civilizations)
  Includes bibliographical references and index.
  ISBN 0-8094-9037-4
  1. India—Antiquities. 2. India—Civilization—To 1200. I. Series.
DS418.A82 1994
934—dc20   94-29622
                             CIP

LOST CIVILIZATIONS

SERIES EDITOR: Dale M. Brown
Administrative Editor: Philip Brandt George

Editorial staff for *Ancient India: Land of Mystery*
Art Directors: Bill McKenney (principal), Ellen L. Pattisall
Picture Editors: Marion Ferguson Briggs, Paula York-Soderlund
Text Editors: Russell B. Adams Jr. (principal), Charlotte Anker, Charles J. Hagner
Associate Editors/Research-Writing: Robin Currie, Katherine L. Griffin, Jarelle S. Stein
Senior Copyeditor: Mary Elizabeth Oelkers-Keegan
Picture Coordinator: Catherine Parrott
Editorial Assistant: Patricia D. Whiteford

Special Contributors: Timothy Cooke, Laura Foreman, Jim L. Hicks, Thomas Lewis, Barbara Mallen (text); Vilasini Balakrishnan, Tom DiGiovanni, Ylann Schemm (research); Roy Nanovic (index).

Correspondents: Elisabeth Kraemer-Singh (Bonn), Christine Hinze (London), Christina Lieberman (New York), Maria Vincenza Aloisi (Paris), Ann Natanson (Rome). Valuable assistance was also provided by: Safdar Barlas (Karachi); Judy Aspinall (London); Meenakshi Ganguly (New Delhi); Elizabeth Brown, Daniel Donnelly (New York); Ann Wise (Rome).

The Consultants:
Bridget Allchin is a fellow of Wolfson College, Cambridge, secretary of the Ancient India and Iran Trust, editor of the journal *South Asian Studies*, and secretary general of the European Association of South Asian Archaeologists. Her publications include *The Prehistory and Palaeogeography of the Great Indian Desert* and *South Asian Archaeology.*

Raymond Allchin, whose interest in ancient Indian culture and history spans more than 50 years, is emeritus reader in Indian Studies at Cambridge and a fellow of the British Academy. He has completed a major study of the emergence of cities and states in early historic South Asia. Among his many publications are *Piklihal Excavations* and *Neolithic Cattle Keepers of South India.*

Roy C. Craven Jr. is professor of art, emeritus, at the University of Florida and founding director of the University Gallery. Since his first visit to India as a U.S. Air Force photographer in 1942, he has pursued his interest in the art of the area and in photography. His images have been utilized in museum displays around the world as well as in his own publications and those of others.

Jonathan Mark Kenoyer, assistant professor of anthropology at the University of Wisconsin at Madison, was born and raised in India. Concentrating in Indus Valley archaeology and ancient technology, he has more than two decades of field experience in India and Pakistan, including time as codirector and field director of the excavations at Harappa, Pakistan.

Jim G. Shaffer, author of scores of works on the pre- and protohistoric cultures of South and Southwest Asia, is associate professor of anthropology at Case Western Reserve University in Cleveland. Almost yearly since 1970, he has done extensive archaeological fieldwork in Afghanistan, Pakistan, and India.

Doris Meth Srinivasan is associate professorial lecturer in the Department of Art at George Washington University in Washington, D.C. A specialist in South Asian art, she has published numerous works in the field, including the two-volume *Origins of Divine Multiplicity in Indian Art: Meaning and Form.*

This volume is one in a series that explores the worlds of the past, using the finds of archaeologists and other scientists to bring ancient peoples and their cultures vividly to life.

ANCIENT INDIA: LAND OF MYSTERY

By the Editors of Time-Life Books

TIME-LIFE BOOKS, ALEXANDRIA, VIRGINIA

CONTENTS

A Buddhist stupa built in the second century AD looming behind them, the brick ruins of the third-millennium-BC city of Mohenjodaro seem to glow in the changing light of day. An Indian archaeologist found the city's remains in 1919 while investigating the stupa. Mohenjodaro's discovery led to the revelation that a great urban civilization, the Harappan, had once flourished in the Indus Valley of ancient India.

A LOST CIVILIZATION 5,000 YEARS IN THE MAKING

A typical terra cotta from Mohenjodaro, believed by some to represent a mother goddess, wears a flamboyant headdress with two cups. Soot traces found in the cups of similar pieces suggest such figurines may have held burning oil or incense.

Indian archaeology was still in its infancy when Sir Alexander Cunningham, director general of the newly formed Archaeological Survey of India, revisited the ruins of Harappa in the winter of 1873. Cunningham had first viewed the site—a two-and-a-half-mile expanse of crumbling mud brick on the flood plain of the Ravi River in the Indus Valley—20 years before, after reading about it in the journals of an inveterate wanderer and British Army deserter known as Charles Masson. Masson, a mysterious figure whose real name was James Lewis, had come upon Harappa in 1826 while traveling through the marshy woodlands of what is today the Punjab region of Pakistan. Dominating the site, wrote Masson, was a "ruinous brick castle" and an "irregular rocky height, crowned with remains of buildings, in fragments of walls, with niches, after the eastern manner. The walls and towers of the castle are remarkably high, though, from having been long deserted, they exhibit in some parts the ravages of time and decay."

Earlier, Cunningham had found the site largely as Masson had described it; now, he could detect no trace of a castle. Railroad workers laying track for the recently completed Lahore-Multan line had pillaged Harappa's finely molded brick for track-bed ballast. Indeed, inspection of the rail line revealed that enough brick had been filched from Harappa and other ancient ruins to lay some 100 miles of track.

9

In hopes of salvaging what remained of the vast settlement, Cunningham initiated excavations. The lamentable condition of the vandalized ruins made work difficult, however, and the dig was cut short. The effort yielded but one noteworthy find: a square seal of the type used by the ancient Harappans to imprint their distinctive identifying "signatures" in dabs of wet clay. Made of black soapstone, the seal was engraved with the image of a bull—minus the hump characteristic of the Indian Brahman bull, or zebu—framed by six characters of an unknown script. The alien appearance of the animal and the strange writing, so unlike India's native Sanskrit, led Cunningham to propose that the seal was foreign.

Cunningham devoted little attention to Harappa thereafter, and in 1885, following a long career in India, he retired. Not until 1914 did a successor, classical scholar and archaeologist Sir John Marshall, resurrect the site by ordering its formal survey. World War I intervened, and it was not until 1920 that Archaeological Survey staff

An aerial photograph captures the so-called citadel of Mohenjodaro. Atop the citadel is a second-century-AD Buddhist stupa (center, left), *an oddity among the nearby third-millennium-BC Harappan structures, including the ones dubbed the Great Bath* (center, right) *and the Granary* (center, far right) *by early archaeologists.*

member Rai Bahadur Daya Ram Sahni resumed excavation at Harappa, picking up where Cunningham had left off. The work, as before, was grudging in its rewards, and by the end of the season, Sahni had only two seals to show for his labors.

Marshall's tentative interest in Harappa might have ended there had it not been for a fortuitous discovery made the year before. In 1919 R. D. Banerji, one of Marshall's Indian staffers, had been scouting the arid wastes along the southern portion of the Indus River when he encountered an ancient Buddhist stupa, or mound, at a place called Mohenjodaro, located about 350 miles south of Harappa. Clustered about the stupa, as far as the eye could see, were mounds of crumbling brick—the remains, Banerji surmised, of a once flourishing metropolis.

A trial dig disclosed four distinct settlement layers beneath the stupa. Coins found in the upper layer fixed its date to the second century AD. The remaining levels offered no readily datable clues. In the lower levels, however—representing a period clearly remote from the first—Banerji uncovered bits of engraved copper and three fired soapstone seals. One seal bore the image of a unicorn, and all three had been inscribed with the same odd pictographic script.

Banerji immediately thought of Cunningham's Harappan seal. It, too, had been found amid an ancient city of brick—albeit a city located hundreds of miles to the north. Could there be a connection? To find out, Marshall had the seals from Mohenjodaro transferred to his headquarters where he could compare them with those from Harappa. "That the finds from the two sites belonged to the same stage of culture and approximately to the same age," he later wrote, "and that they were totally distinct from anything previously known to us in India was at once evident." Their age, however, remained a mystery.

In 1924, on the chance that the international archaeological community might be able to shed some light on the antiquity and origins of the seals, Marshall submitted pictures of the artifacts to the *Illustrated London News*, a favorite sounding board for British archaeologists of the day. In an accompanying report, Marshall noted how significant the Archaeological Survey of India considered their discovery: "Not often has it been given to archaeologists, as it was given to Schliemann at Tiryns and Mycenae, to light upon the remains of a long forgotten civilization. It looks, however, at this moment, as if we are on the threshold of such a discovery in the plains of the Indus. Up to the present our knowledge of Indian antiquities has carried us back hardly further than the third century before Christ. Now, however, there has unexpectedly been unearthed an entirely new class of objects which have nothing in common with those previously known to us."

Marshall's article drew an immediate response. Appearing in the next issue of the *Illustrated London News* was a letter from A. H. Sayce, an Assyriologist at Oxford University, describing the close affinity between the Indus seals and others known from excavations of ancient Mesopotamian sites in Iraq. Sayce's letter was followed by a still more dramatic revelation by Dr. Ernest Mackay, director of the American Expedition at the Mesopotamian kingdom of Kish. In a personal memorandum to Marshall, Mackay disclosed that a seal identical to those from Harappa and Mohenjodaro had been disinterred from beneath a temple dedicated to the war god Ilbaba, datable to approximately 2300 BC.

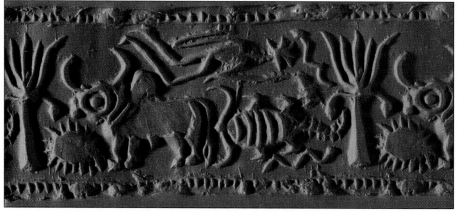

Marshall could barely contain his excitement. Not only could Harappa and Mohenjodaro now be placed somewhere in the context of the mid third millennium BC, but some sort of trade connections between Mesopotamia and the Indus cities could also be inferred. Beyond this, however, Marshall could say little. Who the Indus people were and what they wrote, how they lived and governed themselves, whom they worshiped and warred upon—all were riddles whose answers lay buried in the flood plain of the Indus.

A humped bull feeds from a manger while a scorpion and two snakes crawl behind him and a fantastic figure with rays about his head hovers above them. This scene, whose meaning is unknown, comes from a cylinder seal discovered in a pre-2000-BC tomb in Ur, but the bull image is stylistically like those found in the Indus Valley. The seal and similar ones unearthed elsewhere in Mesopotamia offer compelling evidence of trade contacts between Harappans and Mesopotamians.

In an effort to find those answers, the Archaeological Survey launched a massive excavation campaign in 1925. At Harappa, where plundering by railway contractors had taken such a destructive toll, the effort remained on a relatively small scale. Mohenjodaro, however, had suffered no such depredations; heavy deposits of silt and windblown sand had buried and protected much of the sprawling settlement. Marshall therefore focused his resources on this better-preserved site. In no time, a small city of makeshift offices, workrooms, and living quarters had sprung up amid the tussocks of elephant grass surrounding Mohenjodaro. For six years, it was a second home to some 800 laborers, a crew of technical assistants, and six officials of the Archaeological Survey—including Marshall himself.

Diligent digging soon revealed the basic layout of the town. Contrary to all expectations, Mohenjodaro exhibited a degree of urban planning virtually unheard of in the third millennium BC. The city appeared to be divided into several sectors, including an elevated "citadel" and a lower town. Spanning the city from north to south was a broad boulevard 30 feet wide, crisscrossed at right angles every 200 yards or so by smaller east-west streets. An irregular network of alleys five to 10 feet wide connected the side streets. The same general plan of multiple mounds, with the long axis of the city blocks oriented north and south, was found at Harappa.

Private dwellings were located in all of the various mounds, along with what appeared to be some public buildings. Built of baked brick that, according to Marshall, had been "laid with a precision that could hardly be improved upon," houses rose at least two stories above substantial foundations. On the ground floor, most dwellings turned a blank, windowless face to the streets—an urban convention still followed in much of the Near East as protection against the elements, noise, odors, intrusive neighbors, and thieves. The main door, located on the alley behind the house, opened onto a spacious vestibule and a courtyard beyond. Lining the courtyard—probably overhung by a wooden balcony—were the individual rooms of the house; a brick stairway led to the upper floors and the roof. Windows screened with wooden, terra cotta, or alabaster grilles admitted light and air into the house. Many houses had their own wells; communal wells were located along the main streets, part of a public water and sanitation system unparalleled in the preclassical world (pages 37-43).

Slowly, the picture of a technically accomplished and uncommonly homogeneous culture was emerging. Artifacts unearthed in houses and burials showed that the peoples of Mohenjodaro and Harappa shared the same pottery types, employed standardized tools of copper and gray chert, and fashioned elaborate beaded ornaments of gold, carnelian, shell, terra cotta, lapis lazuli, and turquoise. They lived in well-designed houses equipped with drainage systems on neatly planned city blocks.

Yet much remained unclear about the inhabitants of the sister cities of the Indus. Despite copious evidence suggesting centralized planning and civic control, Marshall could find no indisputable proof of a ruling elite—no sumptuous palaces, ornate temples, or bureaucratic offices. True enough, the buildings on the mounds at Harap-

pa had been largely dismantled by brick scavengers; but some of the structures at Mohenjodaro, while too large for residential purposes, were largely devoid of features that would permit their positive identification as halls of government or sacred galleries.

Then there were the enigmatic seals, many more of which continued to crop up. No one had cracked their cryptic inscriptions. More important still was the question of where these ingenious people with their pictorial script and flair for town planning had come from. They seemed to have sprung into being, high culture and all, out of thin air.

Most early students of Indus culture got around this problem by postulating the sudden diffusion of "civilizing ideas" into the Indus Valley. From a historical standpoint, such notions were logical enough. During the third millennium BC, the idea of civilization did indeed seem to be "in the air." China, Egypt, and Sumer, in Mesopotamia, all gave rise to prosperous agrarian communities that forged cultures of unprecedented sophistication and power.

Out of such great centers of culture, scholars attempted to trace the migration of civilizing influences and peoples into the plains of the Indus. Yet even Marshall, who initially proposed a "close cultural connection" with Sumer, would later assert that the Indus culture was uniquely Indian—founded, he said, in the very soil of the Indian subcontinent itself.

As widespread finds of Stone Age axes and flints attest, primitive peoples had inhabited the great continental peninsula that today comprises Pakistan, India, and Bangladesh virtually since the dawn of mankind. A glance at the map does not readily disclose how they came to be there, however: The towering Himalayas and the Hindu Kush mountains form a daunting barrier 150 miles wide, 2,000 miles

Layered one on top of another, foundations and walls of dwellings built on the same spot in the most deeply excavated section of Mohenjodaro's lower city reach some 20 feet high. The apertures placed at various levels are not windows, but doors from different periods of occupation.

long, and nearly five miles high along the peninsula's northern rim. But closer scrutiny reveals numerous mountain passes, carved over the eons by rivers of melting snows, through which intrepid hunter-gatherers must have filtered south.

From the northwest, these pioneers followed the twisting gorge of the Khyber Pass *(pages 66-67)* and dozens of other passes into the Indus Valley and the hilly region of the Punjab. Ahead, the jungly expanse of the Indo-Gangetic plain swept from west to east in a 2,000-mile arc across the peninsula. Into the Indus River valley coursed the Indus and the now vanished Saraswati River (also known as the Ghaggar-Hakra River), flowing south from the Himalayas to the Arabian Sea; to the east, the Ganges River traced a rambling path from the Himalayas to the Bay of Bengal. Here, dense tropical growth and swamps discouraged the building of settlements. Migrants who ventured south into the fertile Indus Valley ultimately debouched in the Sindh, a hot, arid region of salt flats and dwarf tamarisk trees bordering the desolate Thar Desert.

East and south stretched the heartland of the peninsula, the vast, continental plateau of the Deccan. Its diverse terrain, ranging from dense forest to harsh, infertile grasslands and scrubby plains, was bounded to the east and west by high escarpments known as the Ghats, and in the north by the Vindhya Range. More than anywhere else, settlers here had to contend with the unpredictable monsoon winds—cool and dry in the winter, sultry and soaking in the summer—that governed the rhythms of life. More salubrious, but very hot, conditions greeted those who continued southward to the low coastal plains along the Indian Ocean, where elephants roamed through forests of teak and sandalwood, and fish teemed off palm-fringed beaches.

Until very recently, little was known of the origins and lifeways of the prehistoric peoples who thrived in this sprawling territory and whose heirs gave rise to some of the world's most inspiring religions and art. Since the excavation of Mohenjodaro and Harappa in the 1920s, however, archaeologists in Pakistan and India have uncovered more than 1,000 sites whose planned cities of brick, stylistically similar pottery, and elabo-

A re-creation of a Mohenjodaro house shows an entryway (bottom left) *with a porter's lodge straight ahead and a well room to the right. Conveniently located next door is a bathing platform. A central courtyard dominates the two-story building, which also contains rooms on the far right and quarters upstairs.*

15

rately carved seals confirm their status as member communities in what is now dubbed the Indus or Harappan civilization.

The remains of these prehistoric settlements, most of which cover between two and five acres, are sprinkled over an area some 300,000 square miles in extent—a region twice the size of ancient Sumer. No other Bronze Age civilization had such a vast geographical reach. At the civilization's height in the late third millennium BC, Harappan cities and towns spread in a broad crescent from western India near the Narmada River on the fringes of the Deccan Plateau, northward through the Pakistani regions of Sindh and western Punjab, and east across the Indo-Gangetic plain to Delhi. Other villages clustered along the shores of the Arabian Sea, extending west from the Indus delta to the Iranian border; a few isolated outposts even flourished in Baluchistan and Afghanistan.

In addition to surveying the scope of Harappan civilization, researchers since Marshall's time have set themselves the difficult task of determining the origins of this ancient culture, as well as its legacy to later Indian society. And what they have found in their investigations has pushed the dawn of Indian civilization deep into the past, back to the remote Neolithic Age of 7000 BC.

O ne of the archaeologists who did much to illuminate the rich bequest of Harappan civilization was the irrepressible Sir Mortimer Wheeler, who had gained considerable renown in the 1930s for his widely publicized excavations at Iron Age and Roman sites in Great Britain. In 1944, at the invitation of the Viceroy of India, Lord Wavell, Wheeler found himself aboard a frigate sailing in slow convoy to India. Awaiting him was the post of director general of the Archaeological Survey—and with it responsibility for an archaeolog-

As members of an archaeological team in central India learned in 1982, at least some ancient riddles can be solved by studying the people of today. The archaeologists, from India's Allahabad University and the University of California, Berkeley, were in the Son River valley in Madhya Pradesh clearing piles of 10,000-year-old debris from the site of a paleolithic toolmaking operation when they uncovered the sandstone rubble shown at left.

Arranged in a circle about a yard in diameter, the rocks had evidently once served as some kind of platform. Among them lay the unusually configured specimen pictured at lower left. Centuries of exposure to the elements had cracked it and left it in pieces. Reassembled, the triangular stone measured approximately six inches tall, 2.5 inches wide, and about the same in thickness.

Although they felt certain that someone long ago had placed it near the center of the platform, perhaps for religious purposes, the archaeologists were nonetheless at a loss to explain the stone's significance.

Then, less than a mile northeast of the site, they came across the circular platform shown below. Though similar to the ancient structure, it had been constructed only recently. Six stones rested on top of the platform. Each bore striking concentric rings identical to those on the rock found at the excavation site. Area residents said the stones were representations of Mai, the Mother Goddess, and that members of the local Kol and Baiga tribes, caste Hindus, and even Muslim converts came frequently to worship her, leaving behind such offerings as coconuts and locks of hair in thanks for the deity's protection and intervention. Had the researchers not visited the site, wrote J. Desmond Clark and G. R. Sharma, codirectors of the excavation, "the significance of the archaeological stone would certainly have been overlooked."

Even more compelling evidence of the stone's importance was to come later, when one of the residents saw the ancient rock in pieces. Indignant, he demanded to know why the excavators, Jonathan Mark Kenoyer and J. N. Pal, had broken it. "When we had explained that the stone had been buried for thousands of years and that we had only just recovered it," wrote Kenoyer and Pal, "he immediately paid his respects to the goddess by touching his forehead to the ground in front of the platform."

ical realm grown to 1.5 million square miles. Since Marshall's retirement in 1929, the survey had gradually lapsed into administrative chaos; at department headquarters in Simla among the Himalayan foothills, monkeys often wandered through the director's office and clerks slumbered in the hallways.

A brigadier and former director of the Archaeological Institute of the University of London, Wheeler relished the challenge that lay before him. Although he knew little of the history of India, he knew a great deal about the methods of archaeology and the management of people and resources. Possessed of a demonic energy, Wheeler wasted no time in reorganizing and redirecting the Archaeological Survey's ineffectual troops. Later, recollecting his initial arrival at Simla headquarters, Wheeler would write, "I emitted a bull-like roar, and the place leapt to anxious life. Bowed shoulders and apprehensive glances showed an office working as it had not worked for many a long day."

By 1945 Wheeler was well along in his project to retrain Archaeological Survey staffers in the Wheeler Method—a systematized digging technique that emphasized the importance of excavating a site through its natural layers, or strata, and recording the strata in which objects were found. To help achieve this end, Wheeler excavated in a series of checkerboard squares separated by walls of earth wide enough to accommodate a wheelbarrow; the four walls of each square provided multiple vantage points for examining the archaeo-

logical strata. Now the general turned his attention to what had lately become one of his chief archaeological preoccupations: the Harappan civilization. On and off over the next five years, Wheeler would direct digs at both Harappa and Mohenjodaro, seeking to extend and clarify Marshall's discoveries there.

At Harappa, his fondest achievement was the identification of a massive mud-brick fortification that had once encircled the high western mound that he identified as a citadel. "The wall," he wrote, "is 50 feet wide with towers 30 feet high, and the bally thing can be traced all the way round. The whole thing is pure feudalism." The general paucity of weapons—only a handful of axes, daggers, maces, and arrowheads—seemed to argue against a militaristic regime, however. Nevertheless, Wheeler divined evidence of authoritarian rule in the existence of 14 barracklike dwellings near the citadel—each identical to the next and strikingly like the Egyptian cantonments that once housed the pharaoh's slaves. The presence of numerous circular brick platforms, on one of which stood an object that Wheeler took to be a wooden mortar, suggested that the Harappan workers had been engaged in the grinding of flour.

In 1950 Wheeler concentrated his efforts on Mohenjodaro, where he was soon absorbed in puzzling out the function of a massive foundation-platform adjacent to what had become known as the Great Bath. Marshall had previously excavated a portion of the structure in 1925; from its location and from quantities of ash and charcoal that he found in a series of four-foot-deep brick channels crisscrossing its floor, he had surmised that the edifice was a hot-air bath. To Wheeler, however, the channels seemed more like ventilation ducts. Above them he imagined a colossal wooden superstructure for storing wheat and barley. The underlying ducts would have circulated air through the grain stocks, discouraging spoilage. A possible cereal warehouse had already been identified beside the Ravi River in Harappa; it seemed reasonable to assume that Mohenjodaro had had one, too.

Wheeler named the imposing structure the Granary and hypothesized that it had functioned much like a state bank. Rather than money, workers would have received a quantity of grain in exchange for their labor or wares. Despite the idea's appeal, however, not everyone supported this notion; some re-

19

searchers, citing the structure's square-footage, argued that it would not have been large enough to house grain reserves for the city's work force; others, noting the lack of evidence, questioned its use as a cereal warehouse altogether, suggesting that it could just as well have been a palace, a temple, or a public meeting hall.

Less controversy surrounded Wheeler's identification of a temple in the city's lower section. From the outset, the building's unusual layout seemed to suggest nonresidential use: Access was through a double gateway; inside, a small forecourt contained a circle of bricks some four feet in diameter. Farther on, twin staircases led up eight feet to a terrace and chambers overlooking the court.

More telling still were several alabaster vessels and numerous fragments of sculpture found scattered throughout the building. One, a head of stone, was of a bearded man with a shaven upper lip, narrow eyes possibly inlaid with shell, and long hair twisted into a bun at the back of the head and secured by a headband. Another vessel depicted a similar seated figure; crafted in alabaster, it had been broken into three pieces. Both works were reminiscent of another portrait head uncovered earlier in a different sector of the lower town at Mohenjodaro and thought by some to have been the bust of a priest; in Wheeler's view, the fine materials and superb craftsmanship of these objects were indications of their ceremonial use.

Insight into temple rites came from a close examination of the engraved images on the seals and small incised or molded tablets, sometimes referred to as amulets, gathered from Harappa and Mohenjodaro. Well before Wheeler's time, Marshall had noted that many of these objects depicted what appear to be acacia trees grow-

A digger lifts a rare stone figure, 7.5 inches high, from a Mohenjodaro excavation trench in 1927 (above). Early archaeologists called this statuette (right) the priest-king, based on his austere appearance and the trefoil cloak wrapped over his left shoulder. Similar trefoils, symbolizing stars or a heavenly nature, were used in Mesopotamia, Egypt, and Crete on deities and sacred animals.

ing inside protective brickwork enclosures similar to the one in the temple's forecourt.

On three seals from Harappa, leafy boughs form a kind of stylized arch over the head of a horned male being who stands beneath the tree. The being's divine status can be inferred from a seal unearthed at Mohenjodaro: It pictures the mythical figure, arms loaded from wrist to armpit with bangles, standing underneath a pipal tree; before him, a seated human raises arms toward the horned being as if in supplication. In one hand the person grasps an offering of a pipal branch with three splayed leaves—a motif commonly repeated on Harappan pottery.

The horned deity, apparently venerated by the Harappans as some sort of tree spirit, was probably the focus of devotion at the temple—which may be more rightly called a tree sanctuary or sacred grove. It has been speculated that the sanctuary's double gateway and twin staircases had been designed to regulate the flow of worshipers into and out of the shrine.

In seal images of horned fertility goddesses cavorting among trees—or, in one case, giving birth to a tree—Marshall viewed an early counterpart to the Hindu goddess Devi, patroness of fertility, riches, and prosperity. This goddess seems to have played an important role in Harappan household worship. Marshall, and Wheeler after him, turned up countless tiny figurines of big-busted, broad-hipped Mother Goddesses adorned with elaborate headdresses and ornamented waist girdles in Harappan dwellings. As testimony to the long continuity of Indian culture *(pages 69-79)*, similar figures made of clay, wood, and bronze are part of devotional rites in the homes of Hindus throughout India today.

If the seals have provided tantalizing clues to ancient Harappan religious practices, they have also proved invaluable in elucidating the culture's social structure. Comparison with Mesopotamian seals whose cuneiform inscriptions have

REDISCOVERING THE FORGOTTEN SECRETS OF THE HUMBLE BANGLE MAKERS

Since Neolithic times, the people of Pakistan and India have worn bangles. Such ornaments, notes American archaeologist Jonathan Mark Kenoyer, can yield information about social status, ethnic identity, and religious affiliation. In Harappan burials, thin, fragile shell bangles, for example, would seem to suggest among other things a more genteel life for their owners than the less breakable, thicker ones worn by women obliged to perform heavy work.

In recent years, Kenoyer and others have been using a dynamic combination of traditional methods, experimental reconstruction, and ethnographic studies to unlock the secrets of Harappan bangle manufacture.

In the 1970s Kenoyer identified the shell species used for making some bangles, then conducted experiments to produce the ornaments, using tools available in the third millennium BC. Artisans in the major urban sites, he determined, first removed the interior of an ovate shell with a stone or metal hammer and a metal pick or punch. Then they cut off the irregular anterior portion with a convex bronze saw (similar to ones used in West Bengal today), leaving a hollow, circular piece from which circlets could be readily cut.

Stoneware bangles like the

A woman's skeleton (above), *excavated in Harappa, wears shell bangles on her left arm, customary in Harappan burials. Below, in 1985 Bengali bangle maker Rabi Nandi uses a huge saw to cut a shell, which he holds steady against a block with his foot.*

At Harappa in 1990, archaeologist Jonathan Mark Kenoyer and potter Mohammad Nawaz (left) pack a sagger, containing unfired stoneware bangles, with goat dung. Thermocouples to monitor heat protrude from the top. Below, a 1993 experimental kiln with a thermocouple encases a vessel holding saggers.

one at lower right, however, required a kiln. Italian archaeologist Massimo Vidale describes Harappan stoneware as "a strikingly fine, ceramic material, closely resembling opaque porcelain"—and extremely difficult for modern researchers to duplicate.

Massimo Vidale and his Pakistani colleague M. A. Halim laid the groundwork in the early 1980s, mentally reconstructing stages in the process. The two researchers hypothesized that unfired bangles were first set in small containers, or saggers, and that several saggers were then stacked within a larger vessel placed on terra-cotta rings in a kiln for firing.

Kenoyer, aided by Pakistani potter Mohammad Nawaz, has used Vidale and Halim's research as a springboard for various experiments in replicating stoneware bangles. Since no known Harappan stoneware kiln

has yet been found, they have built some kilns based on archaeological evidence and others on pure speculation.

Nawaz's expertise proved invaluable—as when he suggested that dried goat dung, rather than cattle dung, was needed in the firing process to blacken the clay. As the bangles emerged from the kiln, they were indeed the same color as the Harappan examples.

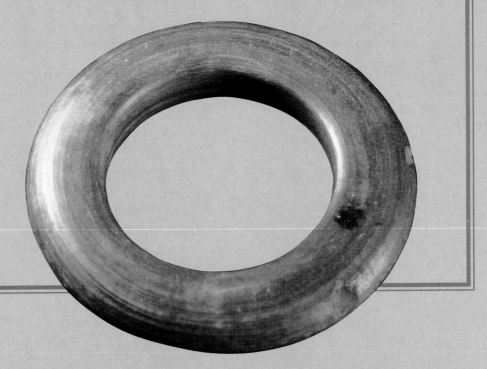

been translated suggests that the mysterious writing engraved on the Indus seals provides the owner's proper name and occupation, along with various titles. But no one, despite countless attempts by distinguished linguists and archaeologists, has managed to decipher the script to the satisfaction of the majority of scholars of ancient India. However, in recent years, three researchers—Iravatham Mahadevan of the Archaeological Survey of India, Asko Parpola of Finland, and the late Walter A. Fairservis Jr. of Vassar College in New York—made what some consider substantial headway in unraveling the secret of the script's arcane grammatical structure.

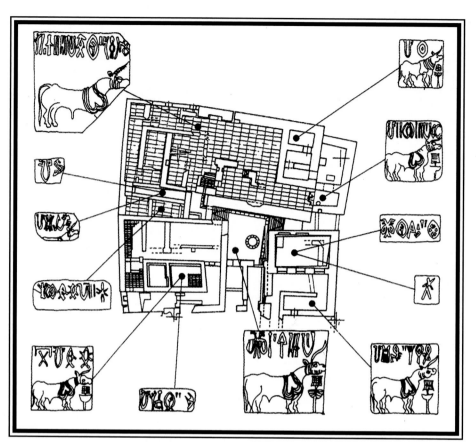

According to Fairservis, a total of 419 signs have so far been identified—too large a number for the script to be alphabetic like Sanskrit, and too small a number for it to be considered logographic like Chinese, with one sign representing a word or phrase. Instead, said Fairservis, it is logo-syllabic: Some signs represent words, and others function purely as sounds, or syllables. Thus a sign may stand for a concrete object, such as a fish hook; or it may stand for something that sounds like "fish hook" but has an entirely different meaning, in the same way that the picture of an eye may be construed to mean *I*. This is known as the principle of homonymy, in which words with entirely different meanings are pronounced in the same way.

In order to identify the homonyms linking Indus images and syllables, Fairservis and Parpola first had to determine what language might have been represented by the curious signs, or "pictograms." Like many other scholars, they each settled upon Dravidian, an ancient tongue still spoken by more than 100 million people in southern India, as well as by the inhabitants of relic communities in the mountainous regions bordering the Indus plain.

Dravidian, it turns out, is rich in homophones; for example,

the common word for fish is *min*, which is also the word for star. (Both are probably derived from the ancient verbal root *min*, meaning to glitter.) Fish pictograms occur frequently in the writing found on Indus seals; often, says Parpola, the fish pictogram is paired with a series of vertical tick marks, which he and others interpret as numbers. The homonymic principle suggests that this could represent a star constellation, with the tick marks symbolizing the number of stars in the configuration.

By such reckoning, a fish sign preceded by six tick marks could be read as the Pleiades, a constellation of six visible stars. On Mesopotamian seals, references to heavenly bodies were frequently attached to names as honorifics. The designation of the Pleiades or other celestial bodies on the Indus seals may indicate that the Harappans similarly traced their lineages to cosmic entities such as the Sun, the Moon, and the stars. For instance, Fairservis translated the inscription on one seal as, "Arasamban, High Chief of Chiefs of the Southwest, lineage of the Moon."

Fairservis proposed that such celestial designations helped to distinguish individuals within larger clan groups. Unlike specific names and titles, which may have appeared in script, clan affiliation could have been signified by the pictorial carvings on the seals. Typically, these featured animals such as bulls, rhinoceroses, or elephants. A seal picturing an elephant would have identified its owner as a member of the elephant clan—a social group that transcended ordinary familial lines for purposes of trade.

Of the enormous assortment of seal images discovered in Harappan territory, the unicorn is by far the most common. To Indian anthropologist Shereen Ratnagar, this suggests that the unicorn clan enjoyed dominant status within Harappan society. In Indian folk tales dating from the first millennium BC, the unicorn appears as a symbol of superhuman, semidivine strength derived from chastity. Members of the unicorn clan, then, could conceivably have been part of a priestly ruling elite. Significantly, 64 percent of all unicorn seals have been recovered from excavations at Mohenjodaro, which Fairservis believed to have been a key ceremonial center. Another 20 percent of unicorn seals have come from Harappa, while most of the rest

are thinly dispersed among the remaining Harappan communities.

Whether or not the unicorn clan constituted a priestly class, it is almost certain that members of the clan took part in trade with distant civilizations. About a dozen Harappan seals have so far been excavated at sites in Mesopotamia and Iran, and four of them bear the distinctive unicorn motif.

Some idea of the nature and extent of this trade can be drawn from the cuneiform texts found in Mesopotamia. For example, one clay tablet, dating from about 2350 BC, boasts of great ships moored at the Mesopotamian port of Agade, their holds laden with riches from the faraway lands of Dilmun, Magan, and Meluhha.

Careful reading of the geographic details and trade items mentioned in the texts, supplemented by years of archaeological sleuthing, has permitted researchers to assign locales to these ancient names: Dilmun, said to be on the "Lower Sea," has been identified as the island of Bahrain in the Persian Gulf; Magan is thought to have been Oman and the lands along the gulf's northern and southern shore; and Meluhha, the farthest destination of all, has been equated with the eastern shores of the Arabian Sea—the Indo-Iranian borderlands, that is, and the Indus Valley.

From Meluhha came luxury items, novelties, and raw materials coveted by Sumer's small but powerful elite class: rare woods and inlaid tables; pet monkeys; ivory combs; copper; and lapis lazuli, pearls, and carnelian for fashioning precious trinkets. All of these items, with the exception of lapis lazuli, could be obtained from within the Harappan realm.

In 1975 the question of where the Harappans obtained lapis lazuli for export was answered with the discovery of a Harappan outpost in the Afghan mountains. At a place called Shortugai on a tributary of the Oxus River some 500 miles north of the Indus Valley, a team of French archaeologists directed by Henry-Paul Francfort discovered a six-acre mining settlement littered with Harappan artifacts. Mixed among the fragments of well-molded Indus brick, a rhinoceros seal, and Harappan pottery was evidence of the colonists' stock in trade: clay crucibles; flint microblades and drillheads for making beads; bits of gold and lead; and quantities of lapis lazuli, carnelian,

Two birds stand in the high prow and stern of a boat, flanking a cabin, on this 1.8-inch-long, three-sided terra-cotta amulet from Mohenjodaro. As testimony to the continuity of traditional ways, a modern people called the Mohanas sail similar houseboats on the Indus and often keep pet birds like those on the amulet for fishing or as hunting decoys.

and agate. Raw stones as well as finished crafts were probably loaded onto pack animals or wheeled oxcarts and trundled south along the caravan routes to the Indus Valley. More recently, another source of Harappan lapis lazuli has been located in southern Baluchistan.

In Oman, across the Arabian Sea, numerous finds of etched carnelian beads, bronze weapons of Indus design, and Harappan pottery suggest strong trade links with the Indus region. After loading cargoes onto seagoing vessels, merchants would have sailed up the Persian Gulf to the port of Dilmun. This walled island town—remembered in Sumerian texts as a place of particular cleanliness, morality, and long life—was the market center through which many of the goods from the Indus Valley passed.

Here, in 1957, a Danish archaeological team led by T. G. Bibby unearthed a collection of weights identical to a set found earlier at Mohenjodaro: Crafted variously of limestone, slate, steatite, chert, and gneiss, the weights came in graduated sizes, indicating that Harappans handled—and care-

An ancient driver carries storage jars in this model of a bullock cart pulled by two oxen. Terra-cotta toys from Mohenjodaro have been joined together with modern pieces of wood and string to re-create this miniature of the Harappan mode of overland transport, surprisingly similar in design to the highly efficient bullock carts still used in Pakistan and India today.

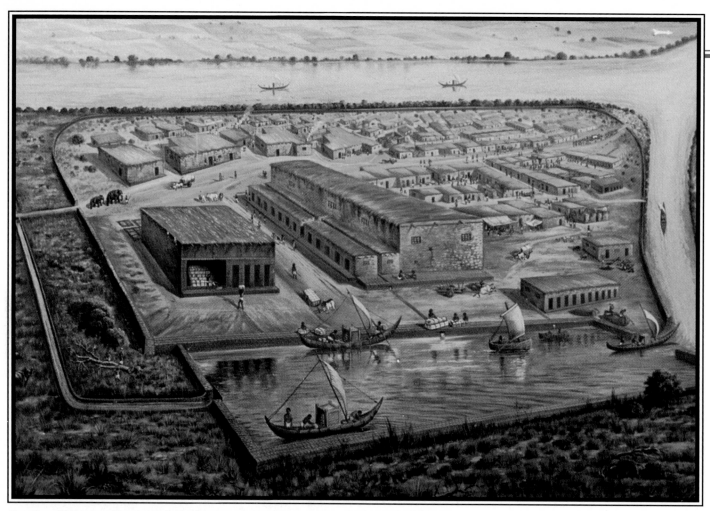

Based on Shikarpur Ranganath Rao's archaeological work and theories, artist M. S. Chandrasekhar re-created life in the trading port of Lothal some 4,000 years ago. The painting shows boats sailing into a dock (above, bottom right) and workers lifting bales of goods near the town's warehouse (above, bottom left). Most archaeologists now agree that Rao's "dock," shown below, was actually a reservoir for drinking and irrigation water, which was probably collected during monsoon rains as runoff from the city and by diverting the nearby river when it flooded.

fully regulated—a broad spectrum of trade goods. These ranged from tiny cubes small enough for measuring spices to enormous blocks suitable for weighing quantities of ore-bearing rock. Over the years, excavators at Dilmun have also recovered 12 seals whose curious hybrid form—round in shape but bearing Indus carvings and script—suggests that they were used by merchants living in the region of the Persian Gulf. These merchants may well have served as middlemen in the maritime trade between the Indus Valley and the Gulf region and Mesopotamia.

The notion that this trade probably went both ways was supported by Indian archaeologist Shikarpur Ranganath Rao's discovery in the 1950s of one of these Persian Gulf seals in the Harappan port of Lothal, located on the southeastern fringes of Harappan territory at the head of the Gulf of Khambhat. Until then, virtually no evidence for the importation of wares from the Gulf region into the Indus Valley existed, though cuneiform texts from Ur document the shipment of wool, cloth, garments, leather products, oil, and cedar wood to Meluhha. Even now, scholars disagree on the extent of seaborne commerce between the Mesopotamian world and the Indus.

Rao also found evidence at Lothal of a well-planned market infrastructure, indicating that the town may have been the hub of an internal Harappan exchange system. In one part of the site lay the foundations of what appeared to be a large warehouse where, perhaps, goods had been stored for distribution. On its floor, Rao unearthed 77 seal impressions whose undersides still bore the imprint of the packing cloth to which the clay tags had once been affixed.

In addition, Rao uncovered a number of specialized craft and manufacturing areas. Strewn about were stone anvils, crucibles, copper ingots, bronze drills, fragments of conch shell, and elephant tusks. There were also the scattered remains of a bead-making workshop: Ranged about a central courtyard with a raised working platform and anvil were several small rooms containing specialized tools and hundreds of carnelian, crystal, jasper, opal, and steatite beads in various stages of manufacture.

Because none of the raw materials used in the creation of Lothal's wares were available locally, archaeologist Gregory Possehl of the University of Pennsylvania Museum has proposed that the town relied upon a vast network of hunter-gatherer peoples to keep it supplied with needed resources. In this way, Lothal eventually grew into a staging area and distribution center for a broad range of exotic items, many of which were assembled into luxury goods for transport to the bustling markets of other Harappan towns, the distant ports of Dilmun, and possibly as far as Sumer.

The importance of such trade to the development of Harappan culture has been hotly debated by Indus Valley scholars for decades. To Sir Mortimer Wheeler, for one, it was at the very root of Harappan civilization itself. As Wheeler saw it, the ideas of civilization were brought from Mesopotamia along with trade goods and were adapted to local conditions by a small but exceptional group of Indus Valley dwellers, enthralled with traders' wondrous tales of Kish and Ur.

Wheeler's theory seemed to draw at least partial support from the diggings he performed at Harappa and Mohenjodaro in 1946 and 1947. In Harappa excavations through the city wall exposed pottery sherds and artifacts that Wheeler pronounced to be of "a variant and even alien culture." In Mohenjodaro, where the earliest levels of occupation had been submerged by rising groundwater, Wheeler burrowed 16 feet below the water table, deploying a battery of power-driven pumps to keep his excavation relatively dry. There, beneath the recognizable remains of mature Harappan culture, he encountered pottery that his colleague Leslie Alcock characterized as "crude, vigorous, and unstandardized."

The idea that these "ill-sorted industries and cultures" could have anything to do with the well-ordered and brilliantly constructed cities of Harappan civilization was to Wheeler unthinkable. For him, these unrefined wares were the products of diverse and disorganized peoples who were later eclipsed by the more worldly, enterprising Harappans. As it turned out, Wheeler was wrong.

In 1955 the Pakistan Department of Archaeology, led by Fazal Ahmed Khan, began uncovering the 5.5-acre Harappan city of Kot Diji on the left bank of the Indus, some 25 miles east of Mohenjodaro. In the course of digging, Khan's excavators encountered 16 distinct occupation levels at the site. Levels 1 through 3 contained artifacts and building structures representative of mature Harappan culture. Beginning with Level 4, however—an occupation layer corresponding to roughly 2590 BC—diggers began turning up pottery and other cultural finds that were identical to those of the "variant and even alien culture" identified by Wheeler in the so-called pre-Harappan levels at Mohenjodaro and Harappa a decade before.

In and of itself, this was not so surprising. What was note-

BUILDINGS THREATENED BY SALT

Pakistan is racing against time to save what it can of Mohenjodaro. Since digging began in the 1920s, 30 percent of the city's exposed ruins have crumbled, destroyed largely by salt permeating the brick *(right)*.

Centuries of irrigation in nearby fields have led to excessive waterlogging and salinization. As irrigation water evaporates, various types of minerals are drawn to the surface and crystallize, forming a white crust. At present, the water table is much higher than it was in the past. Many of the city's foundations now rest below the water level and "work like a half-submerged sponge," says German archaeological architect Michael Jansen. The lower, buried portions soak up saline water that dries in the exposed upper layers. As drying occurs, the salt crystals expand in the porous bricks, causing them to crack and eventually pulverize.

In the 1960s Pakistan initiated efforts to preserve Mohenjodaro, including asking the United Nations Educational, Scientific, and Cultural Organization (UNESCO) for assistance in determining a course of action. A moratorium on digging went into effect. By the early 1990s hydrologists had installed more than 24 pumps around

worthy, however, was the revelation that many of the Kot Dijian ceramics shared design elements with those of mature Harappan culture. Besides anticipating Harappan conventions of form, like flared rims, the Kot Dijian wares displayed prototypical versions of many well-known Harappan motifs: horned deities, stylized antelopes, peacocks, and a fish-scale pattern that appears on many Harappan pots.

Moreover, the early settlement itself evidenced many classic Harappan traits. The town was girdled by a massive stone wall and had a well-planned outer residential section. Houses had been built of mud brick and stone laid on foundations of undressed limestone; one even contained a large bathtub. Among the Harappan-style artifacts that were found lying about the rooms were mother-goddess figurines, terra-cotta toy carts, stoneware bangles, bronze arrowheads, and copper ornaments.

In time, archaeologists discovered Kot Dijian-type settlements at Amri, Kalibangan, Rehmandheri, and countless other sites in the river valleys of the Indus plain. The number of these early Harappan towns, in fact, nearly equaled those of the mature Harappan period. Faced with such evidence, in 1970 Dr. Mohammad Rafique Mughal of Pakistan proposed a new paradigm to rationalize the explosion of Indus culture that began around 2500 BC. Clearly—contrary to what Wheeler had imagined—this urban flowering was not the spontaneous by-product of Mesopotamian contact but, rather, the climax of a process that had begun in the Indus Valley long before.

Naturally enough, archaeologists soon turned to the problem of determining when this was. To start, Vassar's Walter Fairservis and Beatrice de Cardi of the Archaeological Institute of the University of London independently conducted a series of trial digs at settlement mounds in the Indus Valley and in Baluchistan, a region of barren mountains, wind-swept plateaus, and arid river basins to the west. The results of these digs were perplexing. Even the most sophisti-

the site to draw water into a surrounding canal in an attempt to lower the water table. As a further precaution, waterproof layers of bitumen-coated bricks and concrete were inserted into walls to retard the flow of saline water up through them. More recently, the walls are being coated with clay and straw that will permit salts to crystallize on the soft surface, thereby protecting the underlying bricks. But much more needs to be done, say authorities, and funds are short. Their concerns echo the words of UNESCO official H. J. Plenderleith, who warned in 1964 that if the deterioration of Mohenjodaro was not halted, "one of the most striking monuments of the dawn of civilization will be lost forever."

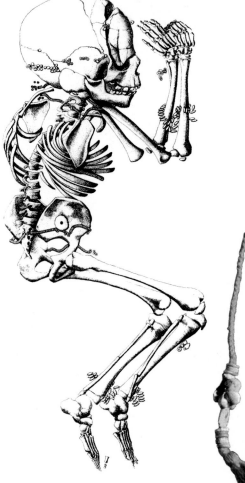

Its blades still held by the bitumen that attached them to a wooden handle, this fourth-millennium-BC sickle fragment was discovered at Mehrgarh. The evidence of various grains found there demonstrates that wheat and barley cultivation had to have been well established by the end of the sixth millennium BC.

cated radiocarbon dating methods failed to record a settlement date earlier than 4000 BC; most of the sites actually dated from the period between 3000 and 2500 BC. Thus, historians revived the Western diffusion model. The immediate ancestors of the Harappans, they reasoned, had migrated from the distant highlands of Iran and south central Asia sometime around the late fifth millennium BC. These people settled first in Afghanistan, then in Baluchistan, and then they slowly drifted northward and eastward into the fertile plains of the Indus Valley. It seemed to be a perfectly sensible explanation, but like its predecessors, this theory too would pass away.

In 1973 archaeologists with the French Archaeological Mission to Pakistan and the Pakistan Department of Archaeology began poking around in the area of Mehrgarh, on Baluchistan's Kachhi plain, an alluvial outwash 125 miles northwest of the Indus River. After discovering a small mound containing signs of settlements dating back as far as the fourth millennium BC, they determined to mount an extensive round of excavations. Directed by Jean-François Jarrige, the digs got under way in December 1974, and it was soon apparent that the surrounding area of some 500 acres contained the remains of numerous settlement sites. Not that they had all been inhabited at the same time: Over thousands of years, it seemed, Mehrgarh's inhabitants had gradually shifted south, successively abandoning old habitation sites in favor of new. Jarrige dated the earliest settlement at about 7000 BC; the latest had been occupied until about 2500 BC—the threshold of what is called mature Harappan civilization.

From a scholarly standpoint, the most fruitful location lay a little more than half a mile north of the mound that had first attracted the archaeologists' attention. Earlier in the century, the nearby Bolan River had shifted course and cut through this site, exposing a clifflike cross section of cultural deposits. Charcoal taken from one of the ear-

Typical Mehrgarh mud-brick structures from the late seventh millennium BC served as rectangular storage compartments. Spaces between buildings were used for domestic activities and graves (above, bottom right). *One grave from about 6000 BC held the skeleton of a child* (left) *bedecked with jewelry* (below), *including the restrung headdress whose beads can be seen around the skull in the drawing.*

liest occupation layers—a village of mud-brick huts littered with grinding stones and small flint blades—returned a radiocarbon date of the sixth millennium BC. Since more than 30 feet of deposits still underlay this level, Jarrige tentatively fixed the beginnings of the Neolithic settlement at around 7000 BC—a full 3,000 years before the appearance of other known sites in the greater Indus region.

The mounds of Mehrgarh thus had a long and fascinating tale to tell. In mud debris unearthed from the oldest section of the site, Lorenzo Costantini of the National Museum of Oriental Art in Rome detected numerous grain impressions, which he was able to identify as two-row hulled barley, einkorn wheat, six-row barley, and emmer, bread wheat. Mehrgarh, therefore, could be counted among the world's first regions of cereal cultivation.

Quite early in their history, Mehrgarh's residents supplemented these grains with animals hunted from the surrounding Kachhi plain. Harvard University zooarchaeologist Richard Meadow, who excavated at the site in the 1980s, discovered in the early levels of settlement the bones of 12 species of big game, including swamp deer, black buck, water buffalo, wild goat, and wild pig. Around 6000 BC, however, the mix of bones alters, reflecting the almost exclusive consumption of domesticated sheep, goats, and cattle—vividly signaling, Meadow noted, a shift from hunting to animal husbandry. By 5500 BC, cattle had become the cornerstone of Mehrgarh's subsistence, as they would be in later Harappan society.

In between the simple mud-brick dwellings of the period were narrow, mud-brick-lined tombs. Gonzague Quivron of the French Archaeological Mission has excavated more than 30 of these graves,

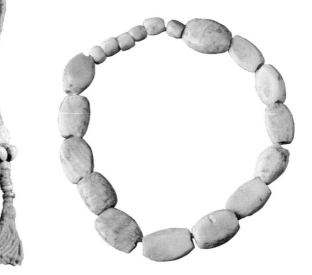

which have yielded a trove of artifacts: bladelets of flint, polished stone axes, cakes of red ocher, stone vessels. Beside the bodies Quivron found baskets coated with bitumen that helped seal and preserve them–once filled, perhaps, with plumlike jujube fruits and dates.

Numerous beads of seashell, lapis lazuli, and turquoise littered the floors of the tombs; beneath the leg bone of a child lay a single cylindrical copper bead. According to archaeologist Jean-François Jarrige, the presence of such exotic materials signifies a Neolithic trading network that linked Mehrgarh with the Arabian Sea, Afghanistan, and central Asia.

Just south of the oldest mound, in a region dated to the fifth millennium BC, diggers uncovered remains of several large rectangular buildings. Each of these had been subdivided into 10 doorless

compartments, one of whose mud-brick interiors plainly bore the imprints of wheat and barley grains. Jarrige believes these structures served as grain storage units—perhaps the forerunners of the immense granaries of Harappa and Mohenjodaro.

By the late fourth millennium BC, houses had evolved into complex, two-story affairs with crawlspaces underneath for storing clay pots. Often superbly crafted, Mehrgarh's ceramics now featured wheel-thrown wares such as goblets, bowls, and jugs decorated with animal motifs and geometric designs—including a rudimentary fish-scale pattern. And the huge quantities of pottery sherds collected from the site suggest that these creations were mass-produced. Sup-

Two gold bull pendants and a gold cup decorated with wild beasts were among funeral objects discovered by workers laying a hotel foundation in Quetta, Baluchistan, in 1985. Other Quetta hoard pieces (dated to around 2000 BC) are similar to grave goods in a late Mehrgarh cemetery and in Bactria, Turkmenistan, and Iran. This may indicate trade and an ideologically connected social elite among these regions, at a time when the Indus civilization was disintegrating.

port for this notion comes from the discovery by Françoise Audouze and Catherine Jarrige of the French National Center for Scientific Research of an area honeycombed with several kilns. Inside one were more than 200 stacked jars. Evidently, they had been left in place when an unexpected flareup caused the firing process to go awry.

During Mehrgarh's final millennium, beginning in about 3500 BC, stamp seals of terra cotta and bone first arise, as do apparent mother-goddess figurines with pendulous breasts and fantastic headdresses. A colossal brick platform, probably part of what was once a monumental complex, also dates to this period. It foreshadows the high mounds or citadels of Kot Dijian and Harappan times.

Around 2500 BC, Mehrgarh was mysteriously abandoned. Some three miles to the south, however, a new settlement, known as Nausharo, arose. Cultural deposits chronicle its transition from a Mehrgarh-like phase through an intermediate stage and on to final halcyon days as a mature Harappan town.

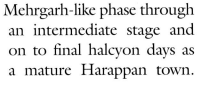

Between Fazal Ahmed Khan's excavations at Kot Diji and Jean-François Jarrige's unveiling of Mehrgarh and Nausharo, archaeologists had at last traced early civilization in the Indian subcontinent to its roots. It had not come, as so many had proposed, in the wake of an invasion or as borrowed inspiration, but had grown out of the long effort, singular talents, and complex beliefs of the indigenous peoples.

The foundations of this civilization were some 5,000 years in the making. British archaeologist Raymond Allchin of Cambridge University has shown that in about 3000 BC more and more features of this later civilization began to emerge throughout the Indus Valley. And by many scholars' reckoning, its most exalted form—as expressed in the grand urban centers of Harappa and Mohenjodaro—took shape in little more than a century, from about 2600 to 2500 BC.

Recent studies have indicated that this metamorphosis from early Harappan culture to mature Harappan culture did not occur uniformly at all Indus Valley sites. At the site of Harappa itself, excavations in the late 1980s, led by George F. Dales Jr. of the University of California at Berkeley and Jonathan Mark Kenoyer of the University of Wisconsin at Madison, revealed a long and gradual transition from the Kot Dijian settlement, dated to 3300 BC, to the Harappan-phase city dating to about 2600 BC. In other cases, Kot Dijian villages never grew into Harappan cities, and instead retained their unique cultural features well into the second millennium BC. And in some instances, archaeologists have found the distinctive pottery and artifacts of these early Harappans mixed with those of their more advanced urban Harappan kin, suggesting that the two peoples coexisted in the same settlement.

As one way of explaining both the rise of urban Harappan culture and the lingering existence of Kot Dijian elements, husband-and-wife anthropologists Jim Shaffer of Case Western Reserve University and Diane Lichtenstein of Baldwin-Wallace College have posited that the Kot Dijians and the mature Harappans were actually closely related but distinct ethnic groups within the larger Indus Valley cultural tradition. Besides sharing such cultural traits as mud-brick architecture and terra-cotta figurines, these groups all participated in a food-producing economy in which personal wealth was largely based on the number of cattle owned.

During the 26th century BC, say Shaffer and Lichtenstein, the Harappans became the dominant ethnic group in the greater Indus Valley. Perhaps through the assimilation of smaller groups, they built up vast reserves of wealth in the form of cattle herds, which they were then obliged to pasture. The need to find suitable grazing lands for their prodigious herds could have been a factor in the Harappans' explosive spread throughout the Indus plain.

Almost equally explosive—but far more difficult to account for—was the apparently sudden demise of Harappan culture. The civilization that built the great cities of Harappa and Mohenjodaro seemed virtually to have vanished with hardly an enduring trace sometime in the first half of the second millennium BC. The questions of what happened to this ancient people and what influence their culture may have had on later Indian civilizations would tantalize archaeologists and other experts for years to come.

THE WONDER OF MOHENJODARO

When Europeans were living in villages and Stonehenge was just being built, the Harappans already had one of the most sophisticated urban water supply and sewerage systems in the world. In Mohenjodaro, a network of wells offered convenient sources of fresh water in each neighborhood. Bathing platforms graced practically every house, many with toilets incorporated. And an extensive system of drains carried away the effluent. The so-called Great Bath, a large sunken brick tank enclosed by an extensive complex, was a technical wonder of its time. The structure contained a deep pool of water at the very heart of the city's public sector.

With such a vast use of water, the Harappans may have been among the first people, as the archaeological architect Michael Jansen has said, to cross the line between "water as a basic necessity and as a luxury commodity, squandering it."

Jansen, head of the German Research Project Mo-
henjodaro, has been documenting the city's ruins since 1979. Because of an ongoing ban on excavations, he and his team have used nonintrusive research methods, including photography with an unmanned hot-air balloon (*above*) and archival research of original excavation photos. Due to the destruction that exposure to the elements has brought, some structures now exist only in those pictures.

Jansen hopes that his work at Mohenjodaro will help archaeologists to revise the chronology of the site and to understand the complex processes involved in the growth of a city. (The original chronology, developed in the 1920s and '30s, was based on the erroneous assumption that all structures found at the same level were contemporaneous.) He has begun tracing the connections between building levels and water structures, reasoning that those of the same period will be linked—an innovative use of an ancient water system, once an innovation itself.

THE PLEASURES OF INDOOR PLUMBING

Apparently inspired to develop urban water sources by the unreliable Indus, which often shifted course, Harappans may have sunk more than 600 cylindrical wells in Mohenjodaro. The structures were an innovation in form as well as supply, shaped to withstand deep lateral pressure. Artisans also designed a special brick, tapered for the smaller inside circumference of the wells.

Engineers constructed the brick bathing platforms with equal care. They raised the floors slightly for better drainage, often ground brick edges for better fit, and tucked platforms into corners or built separate rooms for them. Platforms and toilets were installed against outside walls, where water and waste could spill down chutes, into the city's drainage system. Other chutes allowed household trash to be dumped into street-level bins.

A large work force undoubtedly kept the system functioning, cleaning out soakpits, flushing drains with water, and perhaps trying to keep residents from being overpowered by the odor of their impressive disposal system.

A 1983 hot-air balloon photo, marked with a grid pattern for mapping purposes, reveals the abundance of wells in the DK-G area, the most deeply excavated site in the lower city. Below, one of the area's wells sits next to a brick floor pitted with special hollows, possibly for holding pointed-base storage jars.

A wooden plank or longer brick, placed on raised side brackets, may once have formed the seat for this structure, believed to have been a toilet. But as often as not a hole in the floor sufficed for calls of nature—as it still does today in some parts of the world.

This effluent chute emptied wastewater from a bathing platform into a drain. Some chutes, located too far from the main drainage system, discharged into jars that allowed liquid to seep into the ground but left solid wastes to be cleaned out by workers.

The bathing platform at left and the one below drawn by Jansen both have stairs—but researchers disagree on the steps' functions. Some claim the stairs in the photo led to a second floor; others think steps, like those below, may have enabled servants to pour water on bathers from a height.

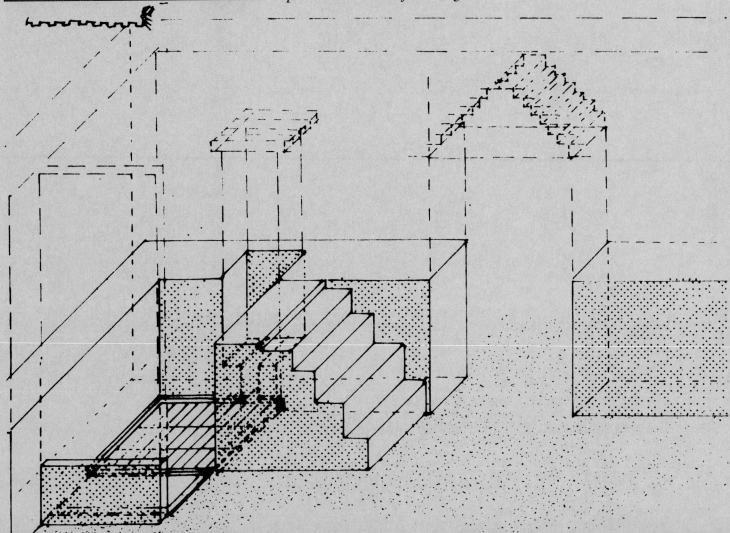

Tributary drains run from several houses into a collective drain stretching along a lane of the DK-G area. Mohenjodaro's drains frequently were set 20 to 24 inches below street level.

A drain on the citadel turns the corner in a gradual curve to prevent friction or restricted flow of sewage. Tapered bricks, usually reserved for wells, were sometimes used on drain curves.

An inlet channel (at left in the photo below) discharged waste from the drain system into a soakpit, where solids settled while liquid effluent flowed on into an outlet channel—set one brick row lower. Harappans used this arrangement on long drains to prevent clogging.

Jansen's drawings profile Mohenjodaro drains. The first (left, top) has a fairly common base and covering, both built with 10-inch-long bricks. A rarer cover of stone caps the second drain, whose 20-inch-wide base is formed by bricks set on edge. Next, a two-brick roof, which was stabilized by packed earth, peaks over an 18-inch-wide drain. Large drains, such as the one at the Great Bath, required a corbeled arch (bottom). Water ran along the channel, while the walkway allowed access for maintenance.

THE GREAT BATH AND ITS CONDUITS

Excavated in 1925, the Great Bath (seen here from the north) is a technical marvel, unique among Indus architecture. A complex of long corridors and many rooms enclosed a pool 39 feet long, 23 feet wide, and 8 feet deep. To make the pool watertight, engineers built a wall of precisely set bricks, the joints only millimeters wide, and sealed it with an inch-thick layer of bitumen (probably imported from Baluchistan). This wall was supported by a second one.

Most researchers agree the Great Bath was more than a public bathing area. It and the bathing platforms suggest a society engaged in rites of ablutions still common in Pakistan and India today. With their technology, the Harappans may have been using a luxurious amount of water for something that they thought of as a basic necessity—in their eyes, essential use rather than squandering. "Mohenjodaro," Michael Jansen comments, "is one of the earliest examples of an urban society's ambiguous attitude to water."

In the 1931 reconstruction of the Great Bath above (seen from the south), two southern entrances lead to a colonnaded gallery, which encloses the pool itself. A double-walled well (center right) may have supplied water for the pool, and the corbeled drain on the left emptied it. In an early excavation photo at top left, a man peers from inside the drain, which is more than six feet high.

ILLUMINATING THE VEDIC DARK AGE

Two of the skeletons lay on the brick stairs leading from a lane down to the public wellhouse. One of them was a man, the other, possibly, a woman. They evidently had been crawling up toward the street when they died, one of them toppling over backward at the last. Outside, scattered in the lane, lay the skulls of two more individuals. In a neighborhood not far away, nine other bodies, including those of five children, were found clumped together in a way suggesting that they had been thrown hastily into a pit. In a room of a large house on the opposite side of the city was a ghastly jumble of remains—13 men and women, along with a child—one of the skulls gashed as if with a sword, and another damaged as if by a similar weapon.

In all, about 37 bodies or parts of bodies had been left lying in streets and houses of the great Harappan city of Mohenjodaro around 1800 BC. Their discovery during the excavations of Sir John Marshall and E. J. H. Mackay between 1922 and 1931 posed a murder mystery of surpassing import, one that raised questions not merely about the identity of the killers but about the end of a civilization and the events of a subsequent millennium. It was apparent that from the time the victims supposedly fell bleeding to the bricks, Mohenjodaro—one of the greatest cities of the flourishing Indus Valley civilization—remained uninhabited for 2,000 years.

What is more, the entire civilization of the Harappans seemed to have been eclipsed for a thousand years, after which, about 600 BC, there would emerge in the valley of the Ganges River far to the east a vigorous new culture, very different from the vanished Harappans—possessing a different language, a new religion, a magnificent literature, a productive agriculture, and a sophisticated iron technology. What happened to the Bronze Age Harappans, and what transpired during the succeeding millennium, were two of the most perplexing questions ever to confront archaeologists.

In the mid 1940s preeminent British archaeologist Sir Mortimer Wheeler, then director general of the Archaeological Survey of India, explained part of the equation—the mystery of the skeletons—to his satisfaction and that of many of his colleagues. Wheeler identified the killers as nomadic invaders from the west, who defeated the people not only of Mohenjodaro but of most of the Indus Valley.

But the mystery would not stay solved. In the years to come, troubling new pieces of evidence would chip away persistently at the foundations of Wheeler's solution until it would topple entirely, to be replaced by a far more complex and interesting explanation.

By the early part of the second millennium BC, Sir Mortimer Wheeler observed, the great Harappan city of Mohenjodaro "was becoming a slum." The archaeologists who in the early to mid 1900s had excavated the later levels of the ancient city found abundant signs of what Wheeler called "progressive degeneration." Among other things, deep deposits of silt and layers of collapsed structures indicated the 700-year-old city had been afflicted by "abnormal and devastating floods." Houses built on the ruins of previous habitations "were increasingly shoddy in construction, increasingly carved up into warrens for a swarming lower-grade population."

Wheeler offered no confident explanation for the marked decline of what he described as an

In the upper layer of an excavated area in Mohenjodaro (below), *house walls exhibit more casual construction and crowding than those uncovered in lower layers, where a grid of lanes and streets dominated some areas of the city. Flooding and silt deposition by the nearby Indus River may have contributed to the change, prompting people to build atop previous structures as water and ground levels rose and the quality of life deteriorated.*

"immense, evolved, and long-lived civilization." But because of the skeletons found scattered at Mohenjodaro, he had no doubt about what caused its fall. Perhaps influenced by his service as a brigadier in World War II and his prior studies of the march of militant Roman civilization through much of Europe and Britain, Wheeler conclud- ed that "we have here in fact the vestiges of a final massacre, after which Mohenjo-daro ceased to exist."

Wheeler found supporting evidence for his scenario when, in 1946, he excavated at Harappa, the city that had given its name to the Indus Valley civilization. There, around what he took to be a central citadel, Wheeler found the enormous mud-brick walls that he thought must be fortifications, raised against potential invaders.

It was easy enough for him to identify these alleged aggres- sors because they had left a written record of their onslaughts. In hymns to their gods and songs of their ancient history, the so-called Indo-Aryan people—cattle-herding, horse-riding, warlike semi- nomads who probably drifted southeastward from central Asia by way of Iran to appear in the Indus Valley about 1800 BC—had pro- vided Wheeler with the equivalent of a signed confession. "Skilled in all manly deeds the God terrific hath with his weapons mastered these

opponents," one such hymn proclaimed. "Indra [the Indo-Aryans' rain god and god of war] in a rapturous joy shook down their castles: he slew them in his might, the thunder-wielder."

Many such verses were to be found in the Sanskrit manuscript called the Rigveda, the earliest of the four Vedas, or Books of Knowledge, that would become the basic scriptures of Hinduism. They described attacks by chariot-driving, Sanskrit-speaking newcomers on walled cities, presumably of the Indus Valley. "For fear of thee forth fled the dark-hued races, scattered abroad, deserting their possessions," exulted another paean to Agni, the Indo-Aryan god of fire, "When thou, Agni, didst light up and rend their castles."

From the combined evidence of the skeletons unearthed at Mohenjodaro, the defensive works at Harappa, and the Rigveda, Wheeler boldly concluded that "the Harappans of the Indus Valley, in their decadence, in or about 17th century BC, fell before the advancing Aryans." It was a neat explanation of the advent of a millennium—from about 1800 to 600 BC—that had remained so shrouded in mystery and had bequeathed so little to posterity (other than the Vedas) that historians had come to call it the Vedic Dark Age.

Wheeler's view of the fall of the Harappans was widely accepted, along with its implications: that the ancient Indus civilization had been a blind alley of history, that the Vedic Dark Age was a thousand years that hardly mattered, that culture reappeared on the subcontinent, in Indo-Aryan form, only with the advent of classical India in about 600 BC. When Wheeler asked himself what contribution the vanished Harappan people had made "to the enduring sumtotal of human achievement," his answer was, not much. As far as he was concerned, it had "failed utterly" to transmit the civilization symbolized by its vast physical ruins. The Indus Valley, he wrote, "has given the new India perhaps little more than a name," while the Ganges Valley, presumably the subsequent heartland for the Indo-Aryans who composed the Vedas and gave birth to Hinduism, "may almost be said to have given India a faith."

A nattily dressed Sir Mortimer Wheeler, director general of the Archaeological Survey of India between 1944 and 1948, kneels to examine an excavation in the buried city of Harappa. His view that sprawled skeletons in the dirt of Harappa's sister city, Mohenjodaro (top), belonged to massacre victims fostered the erroneous notion that Aryan invaders conquered the inhabitants of the Indus Valley and put an end to the Harappan civilization that had spawned both cities.

As it turned out, however, Wheeler had misread the skeletons and the mud-brick walls. And he had drastically underestimated the vitality of the Harappans while exaggerating the impact of the Indo-Aryans—who were not, as Wheeler and many others have assumed, a distinct race of people, but a group of tribes that shared a common language and culture; Aryan derives simply from a Sanskrit word that can be translated as "of noble character," and refers to all who worship the Vedic gods.

There were, all along, both in the scant archaeological record and in the Vedic scriptures on which Wheeler had relied, troubling discrepancies, some of which had been acknowledged by Wheeler himself. There was, for example, the evidence of flooding, evidence gathered by earlier archaeologists who had, as Wheeler put it, "unhappily recorded their observations with a baffling inadequacy." There was the vexing vagueness of the Rigveda, which after all had been composed centuries after the Harappan cities and towns had been abandoned. Its flowery descriptions of people, places, and battles gave few clues to their actual identity, location, or time. And, perhaps most difficult for Wheeler, the archaeological record of the supposedly invaded Harappan cities yielded no sign of military equipment—either defensive armor or offensive weapons—or of Indo-Aryan invaders' bodies.

Beginning in the mid 1960s Wheeler's hypothesis began to come under fire. George F. Dales Jr., later director of the U.S. Harappan Archaeological Project, after a detailed study of the skeletons that had been critical in Wheeler's thinking, scoffed at the notion that they implied a massacre had taken place. "Not a single body," Dales wrote in 1964, "was found within the area of the fortified citadel where one could reasonably expect the final defense of this thriving capital city to have been made."

Moreover, after a closer look at the rather carelessly documented archaeological evidence associated with the skeletons, Dales declared that "there is no conclusive proof that they all even belong to the same period." Even the defensive walls of Harappa that Wheeler had personally excavated and interpreted came into question. They appeared to other analysts to have been defenses not against military forces, but primarily against rising waters.

An even more devastating reassessment would appear in 1984, after an expert in physical anthropology, K. A. R. Kennedy of Cornell University, for the first time closely examined the biological, rather than the archaeological, evidence—or, as he put it, "the skeletal evidence of the trauma" that had killed the victims of the supposed massacre. Much had been made by Wheeler and others of apparent sword wounds in the skulls of several of the skeletons that provided the basis for the massacre hypothesis. But one of these skulls, Kennedy determined, had been damaged long after death. Another had indeed been cleaved, but the bone showed signs of healing, indicating that the wound had not been fatal and had been inflicted more than 30 days before death. "There is only one specimen which exhibits irrefutable signs of death by trauma," Kennedy wrote, "and its presence alone cannot serve to substantiate the notion of the massacre." Instead, he concluded, the remains may have been those of people who had died of natural causes and whose bodies were carelessly disposed of in parts of Mohenjodaro that had become uninhabited as Harappan civilization declined.

In addition to these revised interpretations of existing archaeological evidence, new discoveries further undermined the notion that the Harappan culture had suddenly disappeared after the collapse of the cities. One example was the discovery in 1956 of the town of Pirak, located 150 miles north of Mohenjodaro (the site of Wheeler's supposed massacre) in Baluchistan. Here was a 22-acre town that had been occupied at the onset and had continued to flourish for the 1,000-year duration of the so-called Vedic Dark Age.

While traditional archaeology was demolishing old assumptions, new technology was suggesting explanations for some of the other mysteries that had troubled Wheeler—the floods and the dramatic decline afflicting the Harappan cities prior to the appearance of the Indo-Aryans. As early as the 19th century, archaeologists had noted numerous dried-up streambeds in the valley of the Indus, and had speculated about what might have caused so many changes in these ancient watercourses. During the 1970s satellite imagery of the subcontinent's terrain revealed evidence of monumental shifts in topography, perhaps related to earthquake-inducing tectonic movements, that around the second millennium BC had gradually changed the course of the Indus and dried up a river described in the Vedas as even larger—the Saraswati, which flowed from the Himalayas to the Arabian Sea, just east of and parallel to the Indus.

By the 1980s the weight of the accumulating evidence had crushed Wheeler's hypothesis that a sudden, devastating invasion by Indo-Aryans had extinguished the civilization of the Harappans. It

The 3,000-year-old ruins of Pirak in Baluchistan (above) *have yielded grains of rice* (below) *and one of the earliest representations of a horse and rider discovered on the Indian subcontinent* (above, right). *Both finds signal major developments that enabled Pirak to persist while other settlements dwindled away.*

was not their civilization, but their cities, that had fallen, and not to armed force. As the Saraswati dried up and the Indus shifted, numerous settlements were probably destroyed by flood; others, built originally along river shores, were left high and dry, cut off from river commerce. Mohenjodaro and Harappa themselves, built partially on huge mud-brick platforms as protection against flooding, were largely spared from major physical damage. Both, however, were inundated by displaced inhabitants of less-fortunate settlements; the cities' slumlike appearance may actually have been caused by overpopulation rather than abandonment. And Harappan agriculture, suffering from exhausted fields as well as flood damage, would have been hard-pressed to keep up with these growing urban populations.

But the evidence that discredited Wheeler's hypothesis and reinterpreted the Harappan decline did not suggest any new hypothesis about the millennium following 1800 BC—the Vedic Dark Age. If anything, the conundrums had proliferated: If the Harappans had not been displaced by invaders, why did they virtually disappear from the record, leaving to posterity, as Wheeler put it, "little more than a name"? How did the Indo-Aryans—nomadic, warlike cattle grazers—create not only the great religion and magnificent literature, but also the splendid cities that became the hallmarks of classical India after 600 BC, and why were these so long coming into existence?

At first, the answers to such questions were not forthcoming from traditional archaeological approaches. Pottery and other artifacts of post-Harappan cultures were not enough to illuminate the Dark Age. And archaeologists could find almost no trace of the early Indo-Aryans, partly because these light-footed herders left few permanent marks on the land they traversed. The clues that eventually contributed to an entirely new scenario were the products of a singular partnership between scientists and long-dead poets, the results not only of careful exhumation and precise measurement but of meditations on the subtleties of songs, the minutiae of rituals, and the testimony of a dead language. And like the history of India itself, this new approach to delving in the secrets of the past had deep roots.

In 1783 the scholarly Sir William Jones, newly appointed (and newly knighted) justice of the British Supreme Court in the province of Bengal, arrived in Calcutta. Unlike many British colonial officials of the time, Jones was genuinely interested in "this wonderful country" of India and its exotic people, eager to learn about its culture. Soon, along with two like-minded compatriots, he founded the Asiatic Society of Bengal in order to study the region's history and culture.

One of his colleagues, Charles Wilkins, had learned to read and write Sanskrit. Recorded only in rare and precious manuscripts, and spoken and understood only by the priestly Brahmins who guarded its secrets closely, Sanskrit was the holy language of the Hindus, the language in which their Indo-Aryan ancestors had set down the religion's earliest sacred texts—the four Vedas, beginning with the Rigveda that Wheeler would rely on for accounts of invading horsemen. In 1784 the Asiatic Society published Wilkins's translation of the Bhagavad Gita, a philosophical text that addressed the question of duty and good works. This work was a portion of an epic poem called the Mahabharata, which was composed in about 800 BC. The first Sanskrit work to appear in English, the Bhagavad Gita quickly became an immensely popular classic throughout the world, and is often compared with the *Iliad*, the ancient Greek poet Homer's account of the Trojan War.

Jones, meanwhile, had set about the tedious business of learning the complex language himself. Before long, he began to notice striking parallels between Sanskrit words and their counterparts in Greek and Latin. And in February of 1786, he announced to the Asiatic Society his startling theory that Sanskrit, Greek, and Latin dis-

Freed from the soil, a section of the second-millennium, four-mile-long wall of Kaushambi dwarfs a worker inching up its incline. Located in the Ganges Valley, the city is unique in the area for having such ramparts. It may have been founded by people from the Indus Valley as the Harappan civilization waned. Kaushambi is mentioned in two ancient sources: the Vedas, reflecting the beliefs of the mid-second-millennium-BC Aryans; and the Mahabharata, the Sanskrit epic of dynastic struggle and civil strife in the 10th century BC.

played so many similarities among their verbs and grammatical forms that "no philologer could examine them all without believing them to have sprung from *some common source*, which perhaps no longer exists." Then he went even further, to say that many other languages must have evolved from this common source, including German and Celtic. Jones had discovered what would come to be known as the Indo-European family of languages, and he had also launched, almost single-handedly, the new field of comparative philology.

For the next eight years, Jones eagerly read, translated, and investigated the ancient works of the Indo-Aryans. By the time of his death in 1794, at the age of 48, he had precipitated a dramatic intensification of interest in Sanskrit literature, not only in India but in Europe as well. And the language of that literature offered to subsequent generations of scholars tantalizing clues about the origins and history of its Indo-Aryan authors.

"Words last as long as bones," commented the Genevan scholar Adolphe Pictet in 1859. Having studied languages, philosophy, and natural history in France, Germany, and England, Pictet sought to capture the Indo-Aryans in the nets of language. "Just as a tooth implicitly contains parts of an animal's history, a single word can lead to the whole series of ideas associated with its formation. Thus the name *linguistic paleontology* is ideally suited to the science we have in mind."

Now, while archaeologists mused over sherds of pottery, philologists learned to wring information from single words. By comparing, for example, the strikingly similar names for the birch tree found in Sanskrit, German, Lithuanian, Old Slavonic, and English, philologists concluded that the language from which all these tongues derived must have contained a word that meant, and sounded similar to the words for, "birch." This implied, of course, that the original Indo-Aryan homeland was a place where birch trees grew. By developing a list of such common terms—for such things as horses, cows, sheep, and goats—students of the language were able to infer a number of facts about the culture and surroundings of the pre-Aryan people.

Gradually, a consensus emerged among researchers that the predecessors of the Indo-Aryans had lived in the steppes of Eurasia, somewhere between present-day southern Russia and western Turkey. There, speaking a hypothetical language known as proto-Indo-European, they had domesticated the horse, become expert

THE GHOSTS OF ANCIENT CHARIOTS

The Aryan heritage of India lives on in many ways, and not least of these is the Rigveda, one of the world's oldest religious texts, composed in the second millennium BC. This collection of hymns sings the praises of the gods and celebrates, among other things, the chariot and the horse as a provider of milk, meat, and transportation. Now, Russian and Kazakh archaeologists aided by American and British specialists have turned their attention to the northern steppes of central Asia in an attempt to shed light not only on the area's ancient inhabitants but also on the evolution of the chariot.

Long thought to have arisen in the Middle East, the chariot may well have been invented instead on the steppes at least 4,000 years ago by the pastoralists who lived there. These people are believed to have been the first to tame and ride the horse, and they may also have invented the wheel. Initially solid wooden disks, wheels would have been used on heavy-duty carts, but with the development of rims and spokes, the construction of lighter chariots became possible. Whereas an ox-drawn cart was capable of a speed of only two miles an hour, a chariot that was pulled by horses could roll along at something like 15 miles an hour.

The archaeologists discovered evidence of this development in steppe graves dating to 2000 BC that contained men interred with their horses and chariots. Though the vehicles long ago rotted away, stains left by the wood in the earth have given archaeologists a fairly complete picture of the wheels.

Interestingly, many details of the central Asian burial rituals and sacrifices that emerged in the course of the excavations correspond to rites described in the Rigveda, suggesting that the steppe graves may well contain the ancestors of the Vedic Aryans themselves.

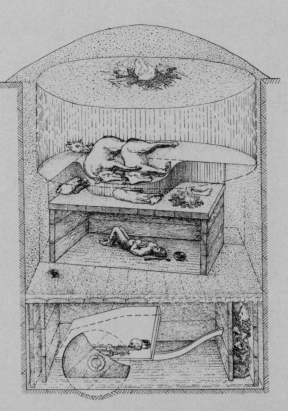

This reconstruction by a Russian artist shows a 2000 to 1800 BC burial east of the Ural Mountains. The tomb's original inhabitant reclines in a chariot on the bottom level. Another male—perhaps his son—is laid out on the second level, atop which lie sacrificed horses and the makings of a fire covered by the mound erected over the burial. Below, working at a similar site, archaeologists lay bare the remains of four horses atop a burial chamber that the diggers will excavate next.

breeders of livestock, invented the spoked wheel and the horse-drawn chariot. They had learned to make weapons and utensils of copper and bronze. And some had moved restlessly eastward and southward, eventually entering the Indian subcontinent.

It was the legacy of their words, as well as their artifacts, that announced their arrival in India. Researchers detected, in the modern Indo-Aryan dialects of the subcontinent, traces of an ancient, possibly pre-Sanskritic Indo-European language, which they differentiated from the relict words preserved in the languages spoken in the northern mountains. This linguistic evidence suggested that several waves of Indo-Aryan migration into India had taken place, including one that occurred prior to or approximately coinciding with the precipitous decline of the Harappan cities. Others followed as many as six centuries later.

Scholars had been poring over Sanskrit literature since the time that Charles Wilkins and Sir William Jones had first unveiled it to Western eyes. The core of these works, the four Vedas and two epic poems, were unique in that they offered written information about ancient time from which no other decipherable writing had survived. But they were also problematic historical records, because they mingled mythic and historic elements without distinction.

The first of the four Vedas was the Rigveda, containing 1,017 hymns that probably were initially codified during the first half of the second millennium BC. These works of poetry, expressing awe at the mysteries of life and the universe, were eventually compiled in a standard form by Brahmins, and thereafter passed on orally from generation to generation. They were not set down in written form until much later, and the earliest known text dates to the 14th century AD, well into India's historical era.

Along with the Rigveda, there are two supplemental works, the Yajurveda and the Samaveda, that provide detailed instructions and formulas for sacrifices and the recitation of hymns. Sometime later came the Atharvaveda, which includes magical incantations for controlling the many new demons and diseases that the Indo-Aryans encountered as they made their way throughout the subcontinent. After the four Vedas, there appeared the two epic poems, the Ramayana and the Mahabharata. The Vedas have come to be considered divine revelations of metaphysical truth; the epics are seen as guides to moral conduct.

The Vedic poetry and religious meditations offered uncertain

IMMORTAL WORDS OF THE RIGVEDA

The Sanskrit hymns of the ancient Rigveda tell of much more than warring gods and Indo-Aryan assaults on fortified cities and settlements. They speak also to universal religious and philosophical concerns, and of more down-to-earth matters as well. Here, as translated by Wendy Doniger (O'Flaherty), who is professor of the history of religions and Indian studies at the University of Chicago Divinity School, are five selections that illustrate the range and lyric beauty of this intriguing work.

The Waters of Life

Waters, you are the ones who bring us the life force.

Help us to find nourishment so that we may look upon great joy.

Let us share in the most delicious sap that you have, as if you were loving mothers.

The Gambler's Lament

She did not quarrel with me or get angry; she was kind to my friends and to me. Because of a losing throw of the dice I have driven away a devoted wife.

My wife's mother hates me, and my wife pushes me away; the man in trouble finds no one with sympathy. They all say, "I find a gambler as useless as an old horse that someone wants to sell."

Other men fondle the wife of a man whose possessions have been coveted by the plundering dice. His father, mother, and brothers all say of him, "We do not know him. Tie him up and take him away."

The Healing Plants

The tawny plants were born in the ancient times, three ages before the gods; now I will meditate upon their hundred and seven forms.

Mothers, you have a hundred forms and a thousand growths. You who have a hundred ways of working, make this man whole for me.

Be joyful, you plants that bear flowers and those that bear fruit. Like mares that win the race together, the growing plants will carry us across.

Sky and Earth

Sky and earth, these two who are good for everyone, hold the Order and bear the poet of space. Between the two goddesses, the two bowls that give birth magnificently, the pure sun god moves according to the laws of nature.

Wide and roomy, strong and inexhaustible, the father and mother protect the universe. The two world-halves are as bold as two wonderful girls when their father dresses them in shapes and colors.

The Triumphant Wife

There the sun has risen, and here my good fortune has risen. Being a clever woman, and able to triumph, I have triumphed over my husband.

I am the banner; I am the head. I am the formidable one who has the deciding word. My husband will obey my will alone, as I emerge triumphant.

My sons kill their enemies and my daughter is an empress, and I am completely victorious. My voice is supreme in my husband's ears....

Without rival wives, killer of rival wives, victorious and pre-eminent, I have grabbed for myself the attraction of the other women as if it were the wealth of flighty women.

I have conquered and become pre-eminent over these rival wives, so that I may rule as empress over this hero and over the people.

footing to archaeologists in search of objective truths such as specific dates and locations. While interesting as literature, the accounts were worthless to archaeologists unless the events they described could be fixed in time and place.

The first such link between poetry and history was discovered by the same man who had unlocked the literature, Sir William Jones. The key lay in Jones's chance discovery of an alternate name for the Son River, which flowed into the Ganges well to the east of a city called Patna. Jones already knew several key facts: that the confluence of the Son and the Ganges had once been at Patna but had shifted eastward, and that the city's ancient name had been Pataliputra. Thus when he came across a reference in the Sanskrit literature to the Son as the "golden-armed" river, or Hiranyabahu, he understood the significance of what he was seeing as few others could have.

Jones had been reviewing classical Greek literature, looking for a link with the events described in the Sanskrit writings. He thought the best chance of a common reference might be Alexander the Great's invasion of the Punjab in 326 BC, an event well documented in Greek. As it turned out, however, the aggression was not even mentioned in the Sanskrit texts. Jones did find, however, that a Greek ambassador named Megasthenes, who served one of Alexander's successors, had written extensively about the court of a king named Sandracottus and his royal city, Palibothra, at the confluence of the Ganges and the Erranaboas Rivers. If he had identified the Son River, one could have argued for equating his Palibothra and the ancient Pataliputra. But his word Erranaboas bore no resemblance to the Son River—until Jones's discovery that it had also been known as the Hiranyabahu.

Further research revealed that at the time of Megasthenes, the city of Pataliputra/Palibothra had been ruled by a king known in the Vedic literature as Chandragupta, which correlated with Sandraguptos, another rendering of Megasthenes' Sandracottus. From what was known about the reign of Megasthenes' emperor, Seleucus Nicator, the date of Chandragupta Maurya's ascension to the throne could be fixed between 325 and 313 BC. From this foundation, using the lists of kings in the Vedic literature, some of the period's later chronology could be worked out. But there was not enough internal evidence to extend the time line very far into the past.

However hazy the details of time and place, the Vedas yielded to a careful reader a number of implied truths about their Indo-

WHERE THE MARTIAL ARTS BEGAN

For 3,000 years—probably longer than anywhere else in the world—martial arts have been practiced in the southwestern part of India. Known as kalarippayat, the discipline is mentioned in two ancient texts, the *Danurveda,* which focuses on the art of war, and the *Ayurveda,* which describes the science of medicine. According to tradition, a Buddhist sage introduced kalarippayat to China in about the fifth century BC, where it developed into kung fu and eventually gave rise to other martial arts.

Kalarippayat—which means training for combat in the arena—arose among Nayars, a warrior caste that made up the armies of feudal lords. To vindicate the honor of a leader whose reputation had been besmirched by enemies, a champion would fight a champion from the opposing side until one died in a keenly fought battle of wits and strength.

The Nayars' techniques are still taught today. Initiates begin as early as age seven and undergo rigorous training calculated to inculcate self-control, concentration, and humility. They must pass through two

Aryan authors, beginning with the territory in which they lived. The verses of the Rigveda contain frequent references to the five rivers that collectively gave their name to the Punjab (meaning "five waters") region, but they mention the Ganges only once, in a later hymn. Subsequent Vedas, however, place the Indo-Aryan heartland progressively farther east, beyond the mighty Saraswati River to the plains of Kurukshetra in the Doab, or "land between two rivers," the Ganges and the Yamuna.

stages of ever more complex, demanding, and exhausting exercises before reaching the third phase, known as ankathari, or armed combat *(above)*. Having become masters of their energy and emotions, they are now ready to learn the secret science of *marmas*, or vital points. By aiming their blows at these vulnerable areas they can kill instantly or leave an opponent incapacitated for months. Though there are more than 100 marmas, seven are so critical that an instructor can make a student lose balance or consciousness merely by pointing his index finger at one of them.

Today, just as of old, instructors are regarded as possessing curative powers and are considered doctors. Among other things, they prepare and use special oils and ointments for the treatment of arthritis and can anesthetize a broken arm or leg simply by placing their hands on the limb.

The people of the Rigveda described themselves as aggressive, seminomadic herders who made some use of agriculture to supplement their wealth in cattle and horses. They believed in vigorous gods—such as Indra, god of war and conquest, who attacked with thunderbolts hurled from his chariot and liked to get drunk on sacred liquor; and Agni, the fire god and intermediary, through the all-important fire sacrifices, between humans and gods. Of these deities there was a multitude, each associated with some facet of nature.

Through devotion and service to these individual gods—the rituals of which were minutely described in the Vedas—the believer sought an eventual union of his soul with the godhead, the power that imposed on humans, gods, and the universe alike a harmony of birth, growth, decay, and renewal. In the Rigveda this spirit was called Rita; in later Vedas it was known as Brahman. Only realization of this universal power could free the soul from an otherwise endless cycle of birth, death, and reincarnation.

Indo-Aryan society, as described in the early Vedas, was divided into three classes of the so-called twice born—those who had undergone the sacraments necessary to participate in the Vedic rituals. Brahmins were the ritual specialists, priests, and poets; Kshatriyas were warriors, who also served as tribal chiefs; Vaishyas, lowest of the twice born, were merchants and artisans.

As time went on, of course, the Vedic culture became more complex. The later Vedic texts and epics describe the use of iron implements (not mentioned in the Rigveda), of the plough, of a variety of cereal crops from wheat to rice. As the Indo-Aryans increased in number, settled more territory, and intermarried with the local population, competition arose among clans and combinations of clans, and between Indo-Aryans and the native people. These competitions involved the gathering of resources and the application of power, processes that required more sophisticated organization and resulted in a more highly stratified society.

To this end, the top two strata of Indo-Aryan society—the Brahmins and the warrior nobility—found they could cooperate by specializing. The priests maintained their supremacy in matters of religion and culture, while the warrior class took charge of political and economic, in addition to military, affairs. Now Indo-Aryan society became divided into a spiritual and a secular sphere, and each of these became more complex. Rituals and sacrifices were expanded—and codified in the Vedic literature—to focus ever more loyalty and resources on the priestly and warrior classes.

This accumulation of religious, philosophical, and social doctrines, a code of life called dharma—"that which supports," or "right action"—became the basis of Hinduism, which would dominate much of Indian thought and behavior through the coming classical period and down to modern times. Dharma was a guide to the struggle of the atman, or the individual soul, to realize its essential identity with Brahman, the source of all existence. In the countless afflictions not merely of life but of a cycle of lives, one either advanced toward or retreated from moksha, the ultimate state of serenity and release from the cycle of rebirth. To the extent that one was dedicated to the daily performance of rituals for earning religious merit; was devoted to the meditative practice of yoga; was attentive to a learned teacher, or guru; and acted in a pure and selfless manner, one approached moksha. But if one failed to follow the path in this or a previous life, then one's karma—a law of cause and effect that transcended lifetimes—stood in one's way.

The later Vedas made explicit an upshot of the three classes defined earlier—that there were people in society not entitled to the status or privileges of the twice born. As time passed, this lowest class of humans, the shudras, not only were excluded from the rituals of enlightenment but were increasingly regarded as possessions of the higher classes, much like cattle and implements. These divisions of Indo-Aryan society, initially based on ability, hardened into a rigid, hereditary caste system, with privileged upper classes and craft guilds thriving—materially and spiritually—on a foundation of disenfranchised serfs eventually reviled as "untouchables," a caste that survives even to this day.

The Brahmins maintained their position at the top by excluding non-Brahmins from performance of the rituals—it was they and they alone who memorized and passed on the Vedas—advocating their use in every conceivable circumstance and charging substantial fees for guiding their observance. They exerted this ritual authority even over the powerful tribal chieftains, siphoned off wealth from the merchant class, and made sure the shudras remained at the bottom of the social order by excluding them from the benefits of ritual observance.

The existence of this rigid division of society and of power helps explain one of the mysteries of the so-called Vedic Dark Age—the absence of great cities. When the ruling class works in tandem with the priestly class, and its power is exercised through ritual, there is no perceived need for complex civil administration. When the accumulation of wealth is rigidly controlled, there is no role for centers of commerce. Thus, in the society described by the Rigveda, one would expect to find life centered on villages and centers of religion—and that is what the archaeological artifacts of the early Vedic period support.

While a skimpy but reasonably clear picture of these developments in Indo-Aryan society can be derived from the Vedas, the question remained: Who were the indigenous people confronted by the Indo-Aryans and what was the interaction between the two? On this subject the Vedas were dismissive, referring to

Of uncertain date, this bronze chariot complete with driver, oxen, and dog is nevertheless thought by some scholars to belong to the late Harappan period. Uncovered accidentally in the Deccan region, it was part of a hoard that included a bronze buffalo, rhinoceros, and elephant on wheeled platforms. All four pieces may have been imported from Harappa, a center of bronze-working, and may have functioned as ceremonial objects.

all non-Aryans with a few generic terms such as *Pani* and *dasyu*. Occasionally they added pejorative adjectives such as "dark-skinned," or "snub-nosed."

But closer analysis of the Vedas by linguists suggested that the Indo-Aryans did not always hold the indigenous people in such contempt. The Sanskrit of the Vedas, for example, shows phonetic and semantic traces of the Dravidian tongue, which many scholars suggest is derived from the Harappan language. Such borrowings must have been adopted by the newcomers after prolonged, close contact that may have included intermarriage and the acceptance of native peoples into the Vedic religion. The name of one of the Vedic heroes, on closer analysis, indicates descent from a dasyu, or native. And the names of several Brahmins recorded in the later Vedas are distinctly non-Aryan in origin.

When archaeologists sought through fieldwork to amplify the picture of Vedic life provided by the literature and to establish the identity of the people with whom the Indo-Aryans had contested, they came up with evidence that was initially confusing. Most researchers clung to the view that, even if there had not been a dramatic military conquest, there had still been an overwhelming cultural overthrow of the indigenous peoples, whoever they were, by the Indo-Aryans. Certain archaeological finds—hoards of copper artifacts, remains of a distinctive pottery, and evidence of the beginning of the Iron Age—appeared to confirm that view. The temptation to attribute all these innovations to the aggressive nomads was virtually irresistible and yet, in the end, unsupportable.

By 1951, 37 hoards of copper implements had been unearthed in the Doab and central India. Because they were different from Harappan utensils in form and function and because they appeared to coincide roughly with the arrival of the Indo-Aryans, they were assumed by some to be another confirmation of the arrival in and domination of the Ganges Valley by the Indo-Aryan newcomers. But in this case, too, subsequent evidence chipped away at convenient assumptions. Modern methods of dating artifacts indicated that some of the hoards had been deposited as early as 2650 BC—long before the Indo-Aryans are thought to have appeared in about 1800 BC.

Another example of how the search for confirmation of assumptions about the Indo-Aryans often led in unexpected directions was provided by B. B. Lal, of the Archaeological Survey of India, a student of Sir Mortimer Wheeler. In the early 1950s Lal set out to

From the evidence of postholes in circles (above), *archaeologists have deduced that round houses only six feet in diameter stood in the second-millennium village of Navdatoli. Working at the central Indian site in the 1950s, an artist recreated the settlement in the painting at top. The tentlike houses were made of split bamboo and roofed with thatch.*

penetrate the Vedic Dark Age, which he called "one of the most baffling problems of Indian archaeology." He was searching for the truth about the Indo-Aryans, and his guide was their epic poem, the Mahabharata, which recounts the struggle between five virtuous princes and their 100 wicked cousins for sovereignty over a rich kingdom. After identifying more than 30 sites associated with the story, Lal embarked on an exhaustive and systematic exploration.

What he found, primarily, was pottery, the most frequent obvious residue left behind by any ancient people. In the lower levels of the sites to which the Vedic literature directed him, he unearthed a distinctive kind of ceramics—"a fine grey ware with designs executed in black pigment." Such pottery, dating to the first half of the first millennium BC and dubbed Painted Grey Ware, was found in virtually all of the Vedic sites throughout the Punjab and the Doab. "In this pottery," Lal began to think, "might lie the key to the mysteries of the Dark Age."

Just as Wheeler had deduced a military invasion from the presence of skeletons, so Lal and his colleagues of the 1950s assumed that a change in pottery implied the appearance of a new people. The Painted Grey Ware was unlike the crockery of the Harappans—it was made of finer clay, more carefully baked, intricately decorated, and elegantly shaped on potter's wheels. Around the sixth century BC the Painted Grey Ware was in turn replaced by the Northern Black Polished Ware associated with the classical Indian era.

The neatly stratified remains of these readily identifiable types of pottery supported the traditional view of the Dark Age: A Painted Grey Ware culture, presumably that of the Indo-Aryans, had supplanted the Harappans, eventually to be replaced by the people of the Northern Black Polished Ware.

And there was still more circumstantial evidence in support of the scenario. Remains of Painted Grey Ware occasionally were found along with skeletons of horses and evidence of ironworking, which appeared on the subcontinent at about the same time. Thus did Lal and others flesh out a picture of the Indo-Aryans as the hard-fighting, horse-riding, ironworking, gray-pottery-using people who had wiped out the Harappans.

Still other archaeologists, however, noted that the Painted Grey Ware was not to be found in any sites outside northern India. It hardly seemed credible that the Indo-Aryans had brought the pottery with them without leaving any trace of it until they reached the Punjab. The conclusion became inescapable that the Painted Grey Ware was not the imported work of recent invaders but was an evolutionary product of indigenous people who had probably been living in the region for a long period of time.

As scholars began to look at the evidence without the previous assumptions about the Indo-Aryans in mind, it became more reasonable to assume that the people had changed their pottery than to think that a change in pottery implied the arrival of a different people. Since the late 1970s, more and more students of ancient India have come to believe that the Painted Grey Ware—like the copper hoards—had been simply a product of an established, changing culture, several centuries old.

But who, then, were the people who maintained this indigenous culture? Since serious investigation of their identities did not begin until the 1980s, the details remain sketchy. In the Indus Valley, the Punjab, and the westernmost reaches of the Ganges Valley, they were displaced Harappans, deprived by floods and shifting river courses of their great cities and towns but still busily re-creating their agriculture on new lands, learning to use copper and iron, and adapting to new crops and methods.

Indeed, there is increasing evidence that these Harappans, despite the abandonment of their cities and towns and the devastation of their former fields, were enjoying a vigorous agricultural renaissance. Around the late Harappan settlements, there appeared at the beginning of the supposed Dark Age a whole range of new agricultural products and methods. Summer crops—sorghum, millet, and rice—were introduced, implying a seasonal, multicrop, multiple-harvest agriculture far more complex and productive than the previous methods. The resulting surplus of cereal grains enabled expansion of animal husbandry, of human settlements, and of trading.

In the heavily forested southeastern Doab and central Ganges Valley during these late Harappan times, other groups of indigenous people were primarily hunter-gatherers who did some farming and herding. During the second millennium BC, these people felt the influence of the late Harappans to the west, learning to cultivate rice, wheat, and lentils and to breed cattle, pigs, and goats. Thus they gradually increased their production of food and began to cluster in villages that, as time passed, showed increasing signs of craft specialization as well as social stratification. These trends, which bore all the marks of Harappan culture, were well established before the Indo-Aryans appeared.

Instead of the discontinuity suggested by earlier interpretations of this Dark Age, the new evidence clearly indicated a continuing, complex interaction among several established cultures. As the Indo-Aryans drifted into the subcontinent through the mountain passes of the northwest, they first encountered the Harappans in the Indus Valley and the Punjab. Their relationship was antagonistic, involving the kind of hit-and-run conflicts between nomadic herders and village farmers described in the Rigveda.

But the Indo-Aryans hardly overwhelmed the Harappans. And for all the hostility, there were some exchanges of ideas. During the second millennium BC, for example, the people of Swat, a tributary valley of the Indus in the mountains on the border of Afghanistan, began to cremate some of their dead in a manner described in the Vedas, without entirely abandoning their traditional burial methods. This occurred at about the same time that images of horses appeared in Pirak as well as Swat, and the pottery in Harappa began to display new designs that may indicate Indo-Aryan influences.

What was happening, apparently, was what usually happens when an aggressive people with superior military power makes contact with a culture that is economically better off and technologically more advanced: a gradual merger that preserves the best of both cultures. Typically, military power is used to impose order and to reshape the social and political

Dating to the first half of the first millennium, a pot from ancient Sonkh in the Uttar Pradesh region of India is characteristic of Painted Grey Ware, the sedate ceramic style of the so-called Gangenic Vedic Period, 900-500 BC. During that era people apparently spread into the fertile Ganges Valley after the demise of the Harappan cities of the Indus Valley.

structures from the top down, but stops short of tampering with the successful economic forms or the custodians of technology.

This process apparently intensified during the first millennium BC in the Ganges Valley. Although the Indo-Aryan newcomers were overwhelmingly outnumbered, they must have posed enough of a threat with their war chariots and combative natures to induce the indigenous people to deal with them. Then, too, with the collapse of the old Harappan political and religious order, the rituals of the newcomers may have fulfilled deep spiritual yearnings of the Indian populace.

Rather than subjugating the natives entirely, the Indo-Aryans probably incorporated the emerging tribal and religious leaders of the indigenous people into their own hierarchy—the Vedic classes of Brahmins, warrior-administrators, and artisans. Having thus given the more powerful people in the native population a stake in the success and perpetuation of the merged society, the Indo-Aryans proceeded to relegate the majority of natives to the lowest, laborer class.

It was a powerful synthesis, in which the Indo-Aryans apparently acted the part of catalyst, rather than primary agent. They did not necessarily invent or introduce Painted Grey Ware, yet they helped create the circumstances in which this superior pottery could quickly become popular over a wide area. Although they undoubtedly introduced the horse into the subcontinent, the animal was not extensively used for economic or military purposes until much later.

Nevertheless, the imprint of the Indo-Aryans on religious, social, and intellectual life is undeniable. So pervasive was their influence, in fact, that after a few centuries of contact the existing populations, from the plains of the Punjab to the forests of the Doab, adopted the Indo-Aryan language, the precursor of Sanskrit, abandoning their own tongues.

The real triumph of the amalgamated peoples of north-central India during the misnamed Vedic Dark Age was a remarkable synthesis that by 600 BC had laid the groundwork for the rise of

Seen from the air, the 20-mile-long Khyber Pass, a major entryway from the Asian landmass into the Indian subcontinent, cuts through the mountains in the center of the photograph. Through the pass and others like it, in the second millennium BC, came the Aryans, who altered the lives and culture of the inhabitants of the Indus plains and helped give birth to a new civilization.

some of the world's greatest city-states. The American anthropologist Jonathan Mark Kenoyer has analyzed four prerequisites for the rise and maintenance of such cities and has found that they were present in India at the time. These conditions include the stratification of society, along with the presence of networks among economic specialties and social classes, and the availability of a diversity of resources, along with a technology sufficiently advanced to produce surpluses.

The disruption of Harappan agriculture from drastic changes in river courses no doubt was a major factor in the fall of the great Harappan cities in the second millennium BC, and the succeeding agricultural revolution among the surviving late-Harappan peoples, with its diverse crops and multiple harvests, encouraged the subsequent spread of late Harappan villages. The widespread occurrence of Painted Grey Ware is testimony to a steadily advancing technology increasingly capable of producing and distributing surpluses. Thus the indigenous people of India themselves created part of the equation for a new birth of urbanism.

But for all the former overemphasis of the Indo-Aryans' role, it is clear that they had, indeed, made a vital contribution. It was their division of society into clear-cut classes and occupations that provided a mechanism and a structure for the next phase of urbanism. The privileges of rank must be provided by the labor of the less fortunate. Spiritual leaders required temples, vestments, and icons; kings had to have palaces, adornment, and armies; warriors needed weapons, armor, and sustenance; artisans required places to work, raw materials, and tools. And none of these classes was self-sustaining.

In such a stratified society, agricultural surpluses had to be processed into food and moved from producer to consumer. Similarly, other resources, such as iron, gemstones, and marine shells, had to be found, worked, and transported as they became important to artisans supplying the warriors with weapons, the wealthy and the preeminent with adornment, and the religious with holy objects. Routes from the sources of raw materials to the places where they were processed and to the places of consumption intersected, and at those crossroads of human activity cities were first possible—then they became necessary.

The development of new technology during this era of profound change was most obvious in the appearance of the new, more-refined ceramics—Painted Grey Ware and Northern Black Polished Ware. But it was also stimulated by the needs created by social stratification—tools and techniques for faceting gemstones, coloring beads, working in glass and shells, and otherwise providing emblems for the ready identification of rank. Late in the period, contests for primacy among consolidating kingdoms stimulated the technology of war—both defensive works and offensive weapons. Raids and skirmishes were replaced by organized military campaigns for the purpose of gathering resources for the maintenance of the regime. More and more of north-central India came under the domination of republics or individual kings.

An example of how this process worked was provided by the horse sacrifice that became a prominent ritual in the late Vedic period. It involved letting a horse, followed by warriors, wander for a year; at the end of that time the king sacrificed the horse and laid claim to all the territory it had traversed. At the close of the Vedic period, about 600 BC, there existed in the Ganges Valley 16 major states with established capitals competing with each other through trade as well as through warfare.

The great cities of classical India were about to appear, along with great religions—Buddhism, Jainism, and others—arising to contest with Brahminical Hindu ritual and tradition. A great emperor would come on the scene, to unite all the city-states of the Ganges. All of this ferment would be recorded, since by now writing was in general use to make proclamations, codify the laws of the state, and record events. And none of it could have happened without the remarkable interleaving of cultures that was the work—and the enduring contribution—of the misnamed Vedic Dark Age.

LIGHT FROM THE PAST

According to an ancient Hindu text, a queen named Latika was asked why she spent so much time and money placing oil lamps in shrines, a thousand in the temple of the Beneficent Supreme Being Vishnu alone. Latika, who could remember earlier lives, explained that in a previous incarnation as a mouse she tried to steal the wick from a dying lamp in Vishnu's temple. Just as she grabbed the wick, a cat let out a loud meow and Latika fled in terror. As she ran with the wick, she jostled the lamp, causing it to blaze up.

Rewarded for inadvertently reviving the flame, Latika was reborn the daughter of a king and later married a king. If her unintentional act could earn such a boon, she said, the rewards of donating a lamp "must be great indeed." They were. When she died she was taken to heaven to enjoy "divine pleasures" forever.

Like Latika, the faithful today still place lighted oil lamps before religious images, such as the 1,000-year-old sculpture of the goddess Devi shown above. And their motives for offering the burning oil—or incense, flowers, or food—or for pouring vermilion dye onto the image remain the same: The worshipers hope that they will earn spiritual benefits.

While the origin of lighting lamps at the feet of a deity or in a tomb, temple, or mosque has been lost in the depths of history, there are other aspects of the Indian subcontinent's diverse religious and cultural life whose roots can be traced. Indeed, the following pages demonstrate how many metaphorical lamps of faith continue to shine brightly after thousands of years, illuminating practices that are uncannily similar to those of prehistoric times.

69

THE STUFF OF AGELESS POWER

Two of the most important ritual substances in Hinduism, and regarded as such for millennia, are also among the most common—water and pigment.

Pigment is the means by which women create abstract designs on the floors of their homes. "Concentrated forms of mind and will" is how one scholar describes these ancient patterns, which are seen as being imbued with a kind of magic potency. And as a holy substance pigment can be poured over a god's image or daubed on the skin of the faithful. There are indications that hunter-gatherers dwelling in rock shelters in central India 10,000 years ago already were using red pigment in worship.

Water is life itself. Most Indian rivers are venerated, and none more so than the Ganges. As Mother Ganga, the great stream is a powerful goddess, and she is believed to be a healer of both body and soul. Even today, despite the river's pollution, people risk their health to drink from it. Every 12 years, at a festival called Kumbha Mela, a ritual bath in the Ganges is thought to guarantee an end to reincarnation and the beginning of eternal bliss.

Black traces on her hair and eyes, yellow on head and necklace, and faint red in the part of her hair offer evidence that the 5,000-year-old, terra-cotta figurine above was once daubed with pigments. Discovered at Mehrgarh, in modern Pakistan, she is believed to represent a goddess or a worshiper and may have been anointed with pigment daily or on specific occasions, just as some icons are nowadays. The young woman at near right bears witness to two ancient religious traditions: Not only does she wear a red ritual mark on her forehead, she also stands in water while commemorating the festival of Chat Puja with a prayer.

Drawn by Pushkar Mela, a colorful festival timed to November's full moon, pilgrims crowd broad bathing steps leading down into a lake at the Rajasthani town of Pushkar. Tradition says Brahma the Creator made the lake when he dropped a lotus petal on the earth at that place. The appeal of Pushkar's waters is not new; some 2,000 years ago a scholar wrote in the epic poem the Mahabharata that it was one of India's most highly venerated pilgrimage destinations.

THE GODDESS WHO WOULD NOT DIE

Some 5,000 years ago inhabitants of the subcontinent apparently focused adoration on a mother deity now often referred to as Maha Devi, the Great Goddess. Their full-breasted, broad-hipped images of her, like that at left below, emphasized her fecundity. But the Indo-Aryan tribes that gained dominance in the middle of the second millennium BC imposed their own pantheon of powerful male gods and had little regard for female deities. In time, however, the priests, or Brahmins, realized they could not expunge the Great Goddess from the minds of the indigenous population.

Possibly to maintain their authority, they accepted the goddess and other important changes into their faith, which came to be called Hinduism.

Nowadays Maha Devi is a complex deity of multiple personalities. She has spawned wildly varying aspects of herself. She is, among other things, Shiva's wife Parvati; Kali, the Black Goddess, who destroys evil; and Durga, who carries weapons in her many arms to slay demons. Millions of Indian homes still enshrine clay images of Maha Devi as the beloved mother who protects her followers from evil.

With her hair piled in an elaborate headdress and her arms tucked under her full breasts, this 5,000-year-old figurine from Mehrgarh is thought by some scholars to be an early expression of the mother goddess.

In this 13th-century-AD relief, Durga keeps the buffalo demon Mahishasura under heel. She vanquished him, using her multiple arms as well as the weapons given to her by the gods.

In Bengal, at a festival commemorating Durga's victory over Mahishasura, un-baked clay figures of the goddess and her companions are brought to a river, to become one with the elements again.

AN ANCIENT BUT VITAL DISCIPLINE

One evening some 2,500 years ago, a young prince named Siddhartha sat down beneath a pipal tree and assumed a cross-legged yogic position called *padmasana*, the now familiar lotus posture. He was determined not to rise until he achieved Enlightenment. For 49 days he managed to hold the pose, while meditating and struggling with evil forces. On the morning of the last day, still preserving padmasana, he realized the great truths and became the Buddha, the Enlightened One. "Darkness was dispelled," he said, "light arose."

As archaeology has revealed, yoga by Buddha's time was indeed already an ancient discipline. Evidence of yoga goes all the way back to Mohenjodaro. There, several clay seals have been found demonstrating that padmasana and a variety of other positions associated with yoga were already being practiced. This discovery would suggest that asceticism was present on the subcontinent well before the arrival of the Vedas, creating fertile ground on which a new faith was able to grow and flourish.

On this seal from Mohenjodaro, a man sitting on a platform tucks his heels under his trunk, creating pressure that apparently simultaneously stimulated and prevented orgasm in what may have been a quest for magic power and spiritual gain.

A fifth-century-AD limestone image of the Buddha—from Sarnath, site of his first sermon—presents the Enlightened One in the lotus posture. Representing his first five converts as well as a woman and child, the figures below the platform flank a central wheel that is symbolic of Buddha's teaching.

In a pose remarkably reminiscent of both ancient images at left, a present-day yogi seeks a blissful union of mind and body through the exercise of asceticism.

75

A BEAST BELOVED AND REVERED

Elephants have enjoyed a central place of love and respect in the minds of the Indian subcontinent's inhabitants for thousands of years. Hindu myth says the first elephant, the white Airavata (the name means "produced from the ocean"), was churned from a sea of milk by gods and demons. The elephant eventually came to symbolize fertility and abundance. Perhaps it was the animal's size and demeanor that made it the regal symbol of majesty, power, and dignity.

The most popular Indian pachyderm figure is the elephant-headed god Ganesha *(far right)*. Tradition holds that Shiva's wife Parvati created from her own sweat a son, Ganesha, to guard her door while she bathed. But when Ganesha denied entrance to Shiva, whom he did not know, the great god had an attendant cut off Ganesha's head. Admonished by Parvati, Shiva searched for a replacement; the first head that could be found was that of a baby elephant. As the god who is considered "the remover of obstacles," Ganesha is always the first deity invoked in Hindu rites.

Made in the third or second century BC, a terra-cotta elephant carrying riders is magnificently caparisoned in a decorative blanket and garlands of flowers, with floral crests atop its head. It may have been a religious device—or, possibly, simply a toy.

This 4,500-year-old elephant-head figurine from Harappa bears traces of red and white pigment that suggest some wild elephants may have been tamed and ritually decorated there, much as the beasts are today in India and Sri Lanka. Seals from Mohenjodaro and Harappa displaying elephants seem to confirm that the animal played an important symbolic role in the first cities of the subcontinent.

Standing on a lotus pedestal in this 13th-century-AD stone carving, Ganesha holds a bowl of sweets to satisfy his ever-ready appetite while his mount, a rat, plays near his feet. Regarded as the provider of success, prosperity, and good living, Ganesha is depicted with ample girth and skin exuding the sheen of well-being. Also considered highly intelligent and an accomplished scribe, he is often included at the beginning of a book and over the doorways of libraries.

Lavishly festooned with flowers and blanket much like those that decorate the 2,200-year-old clay model at near left, and with its face painted as the elephant head at far left may have been 4,500 years ago, an elephant in Mysore is ready for the New Year's festival parade at Dussehra.

DANCE: AN OLD FAITH'S OLDEST ART?

Long before the peoples of the subcontinent or anyone else learned to mold clay, use pigment or dyes, sculpt rock, or compose words into scriptures, they almost surely expressed religious feelings by moving their own bodies, the most available instruments. Evolution of rhythm and pattern must soon have turned general stamping of feet and waving of arms into some form of dance, even if primitive at first.

Indians made dance and music part of their religious practices from earliest days. The 4,500-year-old bronze statuette below from Mohenjodaro is thought to por-tray a dancer. Later but nonetheless ancient temples are crowded with statues of dancers in performance—some of them fixed forever in precisely the same steps and gestures that their counterparts employ today. Account records of an 11th-century-AD temple at Tanjore list wages for numerous dancing girls, dancing masters, singers, pipers, drummers, lute players, and conch blowers among the astrologers, sprinklers of water, and of course, accountants. The temple enlisted girls before puberty. After their training they were formally wed to the temple's god.

A modern Indian dancer (left) *uses precise steps, hand gestures, and facial expressions that her audience can interpret as a Hindu story. Her Mohenjodaro counterpart of more than four millennia earlier* (below) *apparently performed nude except for necklace and jingling bangles.*

Shiva is the lord of music and dance. His dancing, the fount of cosmic energy, perpetuates the movement of the universe, represented by this bronze image's ring of fire. He dances constantly, destroying and creating the universe at once as he does so. Beneath his right foot he tramples the dwarf of ignorance, and his upper right hand holds the drum whose beat marks the pulse of creation while the lower one blesses followers.

FOLLOWING BUDDHA'S FOOTSTEPS

In 1959 a young Indian graduate student named Sooryakant Narasinh Chowdhary found himself sleeping in a tent in Gujarat in western India, a gun at his side for protection from the panthers that infested the remote area of Devnimori, about 100 miles north of the Arabian Sea. But predators were not his only concern: The 30-year-old archaeologist had put his scholarly future on the line. Two years before, he had discovered two intriguing mounds on a site beside the Meshvo River. The first mound was practically hemispherical, 40 feet high and 240 feet across at its base, with red bricks visible in it; the second one was smaller and square. Chowdhary guessed that the larger mound was the remains of a stupa, an ancient monument that serves Buddhists as a symbol of their faith. They contain relics—small fragments of the cremated remains of prominent monks—that are often accompanied by offerings such as coins, jewels, or other small objects of value. The companion mound would probably hold the ruins of the stupa's vihara, or monastery.

Chowdhary was in a hurry. He had learned that the state government was planning to construct a dam to irrigate this drought-prone region. Worse, the larger mound promised a valuable source of disintegrated brick useful for the dam construction, and the builders planned to demolish it. Chowdhary began writing to the

The serenity of Buddha is captured in this magnificent gray schist sculpture. The statue comes from Gandhara, a region that during its heyday in the second and third century AD produced countless superb works of art.

press to protest against the destruction, and his campaign soon got him into trouble. The chief minister of Bombay—the province which at that time included Gujarat—wrote to Professor B. Subbarao, Chowdhary's doctoral supervisor at the Maharaja Sayajirao University of Baroda, demanding to know why a member of the university was obstructing a development project. The professor, who had already dismissed Chowdhary's theory, issued his student an ultimatum: Chowdhary had a month to prove himself right.

After digging through 40 feet of brick and rubble, archaeologists at the stupa in Devnimori are rewarded with their first glimpse of a small stone casket thought to contain the ashes of Buddha. Sooryakant Narasinh Chowdhary, who lead the excavation, refused to be deterred by the wild beasts that roamed the jungles of Devnimori, saying "I had my mission and I also had my gun."

With limited funds and only two assistants, Chowdhary needed luck. He had not been digging a week before he made his first discovery. Inside the smaller mound, the student archaeologist excavated a square room beneath whose floor lay a small terra-cotta pot containing nine coins that showed the site to be at least 1,500 years old. Within a few weeks more, the larger mound yielded a three-foot-high, headless terra-cotta image of the Buddha; three days later, Chowdhary discovered the head. Overnight, Devnimori was established as an important archaeological site in an area where Buddhist remains were rare. Chowdhary became famous: Officials who had condemned his campaign now showed off the site to visiting dignitaries; the government gave him a grant. Among the remote villages, old folk hailed his discovery as evidence that he was a man blessed by Buddha himself.

If so, then the culmination of the dig three years later made him twice blessed. In the intervening digging seasons, Chowdhary and other excavators from his university had uncovered the whole stupa and unearthed more than 30 images of Buddha, along with truckloads of elaborate arches, pilasters, and bricks. Finally, in the winter of 1962 to 1963, he dug into the center of the stupa and revealed nestling among rock slabs at its core the relic casket over which monks had raised the mound some 1,600 years before.

The squat, round box of grayish black stone, a mere three inches high and seven in diameter, consisted of three parts: the body, a tight-fitting flat lid, and slotted into a hole in the lid, a rounded

knob about half an inch high. Around the side and bottom ran an inscription in ancient Sanskrit. Inside lay another lidded casket, this one of copper encrusted with greenish deposits caused by metal corrosion that had effectively sealed it shut. An x-ray of this inner casket revealed the shadow of a third container, which, after a painstaking chemical treatment had successfully freed the copper lid, turned out be a beautiful globular vessel made out of gold. Next to it, tiny bundles of silk cloth held ritual offerings of beads, small pieces of aromatic wood, and strips of gold and silver. Although its lid was broken, the golden vessel still held its contents of cremated ash.

When the Sanskrit inscription on the first container was translated, it told when the stupa was built—the 127th year of the reign of a royal family called the Kathikas, in about the mid fourth century AD. And one line identified the relics within: Dashabala Sharira Nilayaha—"This is the abode of the relics of Dashabala [an epithet of the Buddha]."

Once translated, the Sanskrit inscription on the exterior of the stone casket above provided the archaeologists with the identity of the individual whose ashes had been buried under the stupa. A copper container lay inside the stone casket, in which another container—a tiny gold bottle—was nested (below). The bottle, claimed the inscription, held some of the remains of one "Dashabala," another name for Buddha.

Stunningly, Chowdhary had apparently discovered one of the resting places of the holy remains of Siddhartha Gautama, called the Buddha—meaning "the Enlightened One"—an Indian visionary who, sometime in the sixth or fifth century BC, had founded the Buddhist religion. On Buddha's death, tradition had it, his cremated ashes were divided among eight tribes and placed in stupas in eight different localities, from which some were later redistributed throughout India.

The religion founded by Siddhartha has become one of the world's great faiths, claiming nearly 250 million followers concentrated throughout Southeast and northern Asia in Sri Lanka, Thailand, Burma, China, Korea, Japan, and Tibet. These believers revere Buddha as an enlightened being whose teachings, recorded in scriptures centuries after his death, show the way to achieve Nirvana, a perfect state of blessedness that is neither being nor nonbeing, dissociated from the change, suffering, and desires of human life. The inner fires of greed, hatred, and ignorance are extinguished—in Sanskrit the word Nirvana means "a blowing out"—by developing personal morality and wisdom and by renouncing false ideas.

Chowdhary's efforts earned him his doctorate, and he went on to an archaeological career at the same university from which Subbarao had threatened to expel him. But his discovery had a far wider significance. It capped a period of archaeological investiga-

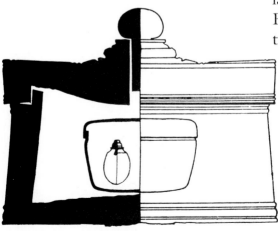

THE STUPA: A THREE-DIMENSIONAL MODEL OF BUDDHISM'S UNIVERSE

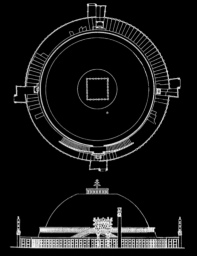

The stupa is a major emblem of Buddhism. This unusual architectural form, which is based upon the ancient Indian practice of burying the dead under a mound of earth and rock, grew into the ultimate Buddhist symbol for Nirvana—the release of the soul from this world into one of salvation.

Ashoka, the Mauryan emperor who ruled more than two centuries after Buddha's death, built some of the earliest stupas that can be dated with any certainty. Yet the custom surely predates Ashoka, as Buddha himself directed his disciples to erect a stupa over his remains. When Buddha died, his ashes were divided into eight portions and taken to different regions for burial. In

time, mounds of increasing size and sophistication were also built for the ashes of his disciples and later monks, teachers, and saints—and even for objects Buddha is thought to have worn or handled.

L-shaped entrances, visible in the plan above, permit access to the lower of two processional paths located between the stupa at Sanchi and the nine-foot-tall stone balustrade that rings it. A double stairway on the south leads from ground level up to a 16-foot-high upper walkway, meant for circumambulation. Atop the mound, a square area encloses an honorific three-tiered umbrella that symbolically links the heavens with the sacred precinct of the stupa and its holy relics.

Some stupas contain networks of walls forming the hub, spokes, and rim of a wheel, while others have interior walls in a swastika shape. The wheel represents the sun, time, and Buddhist law (dharma); the swastika stands for the cosmic dance around a fixed center and guards against evil.

The Great Stupa at Sanchi in central India was built of brick by Ashoka but was enlarged in the second century BC with a stone exterior. The 1868 photo at top left shows the ruins of the stupa's western gate. Here, only one of its two carved square pillars stands; the second, toppled by an earthquake, lies among the rubble. At left, workers of the Bengal Asiatic Society restore the stupa in the 1880s. The photo above presents the reconstructed western gate as it appears today.

Chubby dwarfs, identified with ignorance and negative karma, appear to strain under the weight of the west gate, which is adorned with bas-reliefs depicting Jatakas, or scenes from Buddha's previous lives. Early observers considered the so-called dwarf capital ugly, "but its symbolism may have been more attractive to the eye of the devotee than its want of grace is repulsive to our taste," wrote one Victorian visitor, "so we must not judge too hastily."

tion that had begun more than a century and a half before, at a time when Buddhism, though it flourished around India's borders from the island of Ceylon—now called Sri Lanka—to the Himalayan kingdom of Tibet, was virtually forgotten in its homeland.

During the first half of the 19th century, the European investigators who were beginning to reconstruct the shifting events of India's mysterious past discovered an unexpected story. As archaeological evidence gave up its secrets, so too did the Buddhist texts hidden for centuries in the monasteries of Sri Lanka and Tibet, their accounts reinforced by Sanskrit literature and early travelers' tales from Greece, Rome, and China. The pioneers of Asian archaeology would learn not only that Buddhism had once been widespread in India but also that Buddha had lived there around the sixth century BC, during a dynamic period when the growth of cities upset the traditional rural patterns of life, and social and economic changes challenged the established Hindu, or Vedic, religion. From its heartland in the Ganges Valley, Buddhism would emerge to become the religion of kings and the foundation of vast empires. The belief system would spread eastward to China and the populous nations of Southeast Asia, where it caught on and thrived even as it began a long decline in the country which had given it birth.

As Europeans spread throughout Asia early in the 19th century, they came inevitably into contact with the relics of Buddhism. In 1819, for example, a British army captain remembered only as E. Fell became the first Westerner to describe the Great Stupa at Sanchi *(pages 84-85)*, built over a period of several centuries in a remote, thinly populated region of hills and dry forest atop a hill in the heart of the subcontinent. At the recommendation of a friend, Fell made the laborious 60-mile trek from the city of Bhopal into a jungle wilderness roamed by tigers, where the stupa rose above the trees. Around the

Sir Alexander Cunningham sits surrounded by mementos from his 50 years of extensive work in the subcontinent. Even though his goal was to preserve the ancient monuments of India through "accurate drawings and faithful descriptions," Cunningham feared that some Indians regarded him as an "arch deceiver who was studiously concealing the revelations made by the inscriptions as to the position of the buried treasures."

stupa ran a circle of 10-foot-high granite pillars, standing about 18 inches apart and linked by stone crosspieces. Monumental gateways, which were topped by elaborate lintels, towered 40 feet into the air at three of the four compass points—the gateway to the south had collapsed. These entranceways were adorned with intricate carvings: a boat floundering in a storm, figures dancing around an altar, and had Fell but known it, episodes from the life of Buddha. Words almost failed him: "It is hardly possible to conceive sculpture more expressive of feeling than this," he wrote.

Littering the hill at Sanchi were many statues of Buddha, whose image was familiar from other Asian countries. His origins, though, were still a mystery: One researcher asserted that, whoever Buddha was, he was "either an Egyptian or an Ethiopian." During the early 1800s, however, evidence from beyond India began to reveal the truth. From a European in Burma, where Buddhism still thrived, came the first report that Buddha had been an Indian. Meanwhile, in the mountain kingdoms of Nepal and Tibet, other Europeans turned to the study of scriptures preserved by Buddhist monks. One of the scholars was a Hungarian, Alexander Czoma de Koros, who in 1820 had left his homeland with only a walking stick and one change of clothes and set out to walk to China. Instead, after a chance meeting with an explorer who had traveled in Tibet, de Koros was persuaded to settle among the cliff-top monasteries of the Himalayas. Living largely on Tibetan tea, de Koros pored over the sacred texts and eventually compiled the first dictionary of the Tibetan language.

Meanwhile, in the Ganges Valley, the young army engineer Alexander Cunningham—who would later undertake the first tentative excavations of Harappa—was discovering his true vocation. Cunningham had arrived in India in 1833, and soon an awakening interest in archaeology set him on a lifetime of fieldwork. A year later, drawn by reports that Indian builders had unearthed a Buddhist statue, Cunningham explored a stupa at Sarnath, not far from the northern city of Benares.

Many other unattended stupas had already fallen prey to treasure hunters, who had sometimes discovered a few coins or statues for their pains but generally left the monuments themselves badly damaged. These early efforts had, however, established that stupas were solid structures that should be investigated from the top down, rather than from the bottom up, to prevent collapse, so Cunningham erected scaffolding around the best preserved of the group of stupas at Sarnath and began digging. Soon he found an inscribed slab; more than a year later, however, he reached ground level, some 140 feet beneath his starting point, with nothing more to show for his effort. But the inscribed stone was of more value than Cunningham realized. By chance, a copy of its inscription fell into the hands of Alexander Czoma de Koros, who recognized it as a Buddhist confession of faith, thus confirming once and for all that the religion at one time in the past had flourished throughout India.

This revelation fit well with the picture emerging from ancient texts. In 1836, just as a disappointed Cunningham concluded his work at Sarnath, French scholars acquired and translated the travelogue of the Chinese Buddhist pilgrim Hsuan Tsang, who had visited India in the seventh century AD. While Hsuan Tsang had found the faith somewhat on the wane, with monasteries standing empty and pilgrimage sites abandoned, his account would in time inspire Alexander Cunningham to set about drawing a map of Buddhist India as it had been during the religion's glory days.

In 1861, now a 47-year-old major general, Cunningham retired from the army and cajoled the British viceroy of India into funding a modest archaeological survey of the subcontinent that would follow in Hsuan Tsang's footsteps. As it turned out, Cunningham's mission lasted for a quarter of a century. During that time he traveled back and forth across India with a small caravan, living under canvas, descending on forgotten monuments for a few days here, a week there, before hurrying on in a determined effort to record and preserve as much as possible from contractors greedy for any available brick and stone to build roads and railways.

The world described by Hsuan Tsang had begun to emerge more than 1,000 years before the Chinese pilgrim's visit, during a period of ferment that produced a new civilization and new cities and states, concentrated in the Ganges Valley. In the first year of Cunningham's survey, judicious reading of Hsuan Tsang and other texts took Cunningham to Kosam, a village of only 2,000 people on the Yamuna River, 32 miles west of modern Allahabad. There, he believed, lay the remnants of Kaushambi, a great Buddhist center and the capital city of a king or raja named Udayana, who was a contemporary of Buddha.

What he found was overwhelming: "My previous enquiries

had led me to expect only a ruined mound some 20 or 30 feet in height covered with broken bricks. What was my surprise, therefore, when still at some distance from the place on the northeast side, to behold extending for about 2 miles a long line of lofty earthen mounds as high as most of the trees." He knew at once that this was Raja Udayana's Kaushambi.

Climbing the ramparts, Cunningham found that the city was reduced to a scattering of bricks, but the four-mile circuit of its massive walls, with six depressions marking vanished gateways, spoke to its former grandeur. Among the rubble Cunningham recognized two pillars from a Buddhist railing; a tall, broken column of polished stone, and the inscribed pedestal of a statue he associated with a sandalwood image of the Buddha that Hsuan Tsang had reported as standing within Udayana's palace. In a nearby village lay traces of stupas, one of which had been revered as a repository of Buddha's hair and nails. Pausing just long enough to record the site, Cunningham left to continue the mission that would lead him throughout the Ganges Valley and as far beyond as Taxila in northwestern India, the city visited by the Greek commander Alexander the Great, whose forces had journeyed to the Indus River in 326 BC before abruptly turning for home.

As he moved through India, Cunningham was the scout; to others would fall the labor that would yield the full treasures of many of his discoveries. At Kaushambi, for example, excavations begun 87 years after his visit, under the auspices of Allahabad University, concentrated on digging through successive layers of debris to build up a picture of the city's evolution. Buried near the bottom of the ramparts lay sherds of the pottery type known as Northern Black Polished Ware, called NBP Ware for short, which placed their construction sometime around the mid sixth century BC.

NBP Ware—named for its lustrous, almost metallic shine and usually dark appearance—is a boon for Indian archaeologists. Occurring throughout the subcontinent from the sixth to the third centuries BC, it provides a ready means of approximate dating and comparing different sites. Its distribution suggests that the founding of Kaushambi was mirrored throughout the Ganges Valley as cities were spurred into life by a combination of influences, among them population growth, improvements in agriculture, and an increase in trade. The new centers generally clung to the rivers that irrigated the fertile plains on which they depended for sustenance and that pro-

vided a network of waterways for a burgeoning trade in gems, spices, and NBP Ware itself.

Thus, at Hastinapura, a city that once stood on the old course of the shifting upper Ganges, excavations by the Indian archaeologist B. B. Lal during the early 1950s revealed that a new center was erected around the fifth century BC on the site of an older settlement destroyed by flood. In the new city, findings from the NBP Ware period chart about 300 years of increasing wealth and comfort. Simple coins—rectangular pieces of silver and copper marked with a punch—facilitated trade, while chisels, arrowheads, and sickles testify to the mastery of ironworking. And Kaushambi seems to have had a specialized industrial quarter, identified by vast quantities of slag left over from iron production in foundries and workshops. In mud-brick or wooden courtyard houses such as those discovered at Kaushambi, the new urban classes afforded themselves luxuries such as jewelry or terra-cotta figurines of creatures such as elephants, which occur in large numbers alongside toy versions of the bullock carts that traveled the overland trade routes. NBP Ware dishes and plates themselves were deluxe ceramics, appearing side by side with a plainer, coarser everyday pottery.

If there was, increasingly, more to protect behind the walls that shielded cities, there was also more to protect it from. In addition to floods such as the one that had destroyed the earlier Hastinapura, military attack was a very real threat. As cities became established, so too did kingdoms and republics—the grammar of an

These marble reliefs, dating from the first century BC to the third century AD, are among several hundred from the stupa at Amaravati in east central India that depict major events in Buddha's life. At left, Queen Maya, his mother, stands beneath a sal tree soon after the birth of her son, who is represented by two tiny footprints on the swaddling cloth held by attending deities. In the scene of his Enlightenment above, footprints, now bearing the wheel of law, or dhamma, *again symbolize Buddha. Ignoring the early tradition of not depicting the Enlightened One directly, the third panel* (above, right) *shows Buddha, his head encircled by a halo, as his wife presents their son to him and requests the boy's royal inheritance. In the final panel* (below, right), *an enraged elephant, sent by Buddha's enemies to kill him, is tamed by his very presence.*

Indian scholar called Panini, who in the fifth or fourth century BC codified the ancient Sanskrit language, mentions more than 30 contemporary states. Their rise led to centuries of instability and warfare as new rulers turned to military campaigns for expansion and territory.

It was not just political change that affected India's urban citizens, however: Their spiritual world was in upheaval too, and it was among their numbers that Buddhism found its most enthusiastic converts. Early monks raised their monasteries and stupas near or within towns and cities on whose populations they could rely for alms. Close to Kaushambi's eastern gate, for example, excavations revealed the site of a large monastery—a quadrangular structure around a courtyard, with a pillared veranda and cells for the monks—reputedly constructed for the Buddha himself by a banker disciple by the name of Ghoshita.

For people such as Ghoshita, the ancient Vedic religion seemed increasingly archaic, with its rituals and sacrifice of costly animals administered by the privileged, priestly Brahmins. More and more citizens found its rigid caste system ill-suited to everyday life in the cities, where even members of the lowest caste, the shudras, could amass enough wealth to hire servants from among their social supe-

riors. Though Vedism remained popular in traditional rural villages, town dwellers sought new faiths to match their new situations and ambitions.

The urban sites of the earliest stupas—modest brick and earth mounds erected in veneration of the Buddha, far removed from the grander monuments such as Sanchi into which they evolved—trace a story which itself took place against a background of cities such as Kapilavastu, where Siddhartha Gautama grew up. In 1976 an Indian expedition to a site amid the jungle and mango groves near the northeastern border with Nepal excavated a stupa that may mark the site of this lost city, already several centuries old when the young prince lived there.

Here, in 1898, a nearby planter had unearthed a relic casket whose inscription proclaimed that it held remains of the Buddha. Now, as the Indian team went on with their excavations in 100-degree heat, the camp beds in their small tents filled with a rich haul of jewelry, toys, tools, and statuettes: "We sleep with history," joked the archaeologist Krishna Murari Srivastava. Most prized among the discoveries was an inscribed seal that seemed to identify the place as the "great monastery of Kapilavastu." If, as Srivastava believes, this is indeed Kapilavastu, then the ruins mark the birthplace of Buddhism, for it was here that Siddhartha is thought to have witnessed the four signs of misery that persuaded him to renounce worldly life and to embark on a journey in search of Enlightenment.

Those signs had been prophesied soon after Siddhartha's roy-

The largest freestanding sculpture in India, this 60-foot-tall statue of the Jain saint Gomateshwara Bahubali dates from the 10th century AD. Every 12 years scaffolding is erected behind the statue during the "annoint the head" festival so worshipers can douse the statue with 15 sacred materials, including milk, liquid saffron, sandalwood paste, flower petals, and coconut milk.

al birth around 563 BC at Lumbini Grove, only 10 miles from Kapilavastu in the Himalayan foothills of Nepal. A soothsayer warned that the signs would turn the child into a great teacher rather than a great emperor, so Siddhartha's father shielded his son from all sickness and decay during his upbringing at Kapilavastu. As a young married man, however, the prince did eventually witness them: Seeing an old man, a sick man, and a corpse taught him respectively of the inevitability of aging, disease, and death. The fourth sign, however—a holy beggar content with his lot—promised Siddhartha spiritual fulfillment, if only he would renounce the world.

Leaving his life of privilege and his wife and newborn son, Siddhartha set out to seek Enlightenment. For six years he wandered through the Ganges Valley with a few companions, living a life of extreme self-denial. Finally he made his way into the state of Magadha, where he sat down beneath the shelter of a sacred pipal, or bodhi, tree, at a site later called Bodh Gaya. There he meditated for seven weeks, wrestling with demons, until he finally achieved the state of Enlightenment called Nirvana. From Bodh Gaya he went to the village of Sarnath and preached his first sermon to his erstwhile companions, who became his first converts. All human life was suffering and change, he taught them, which could be escaped only by reaching Nirvana. The path lay neither in self-denial nor self-indulgence, but through a Middle Way, traveled by observing rules of right thought and conduct known as the Noble Eightfold Path.

Buddhism was only one of the religions that arose in India around the fifth century BC to stress ways of correct behavior and thinking on both the spiritual and everyday levels. A sect known as the Ajivikas, for example, won many followers with a call for social reform and a stress on the iniquities of class. The Jains, founded by an Indian monk named Vardhamana, later called Mahavira, or "Great Hero," advocated a path of asceticism that sometimes extended to going without food or clothing—they were called "skyclad" from their nakedness—and wearing cloth masks over their mouths to avoid harming tiny creatures such as insects. A life of meditation and austerity, they believed, would allow them to escape karma, the results of past actions that dull the spirit, and to achieve Enlightenment.

Despite being original in many ways, Buddhist philosophy had its roots deep in established tradition and customs. It sought to change the social order rather than to overthrow it and borrowed for its own purposes a few familiar Vedic practices and deities—the two religions existed side by side for many centuries—as well as elements of even older forms of worship such as folk religion and fertility cults: The stupa itself echoed ancient funerary mounds. With the appeal of this continuity with the past, Buddhism established itself as a potent rival to Vedism.

Evidence of its spectacular success was turned up by an unlikely investigator. James Prinsep, a contemporary of the young Alexander Cunningham, lacked the classical education, languages, and social polish of many of his British colleagues. After his arrival in India in 1819, Prinsep initially limited himself to his responsibilities as an official in the Calcutta and Benares mints, until a colleague's collection of ancient coins awoke an interest in the past that later led him to become secretary of the Asiatic Society. In that role James Prinsep made up for his lack of scholarship with a methodical dedication that would drive him physically and mentally to his limits and, eventually, beyond them.

In the 1830s Prinsep directed his attention to a number of polished, inscribed pillars that had been found in different parts of northern India, similar to the one that Cunningham would later discover in Kaushambi. The first had turned up more than 200 years before, amid the overgrown ruins of early incarnations of the city of Delhi. This 40-foot column was so highly polished that its discoverer, an English visitor to India named Thomas Coryat, assumed from the way it seemed to glow that it was made of brass; when he came closer, he saw that it was polished sandstone, inscribed with a curious, upright script that resembled a form of Greek. Now Prinsep examined three inscriptions from newly discovered pillars in Allahabad and along the border with Nepal, and he soon realized that all were strikingly similar. Beyond that, however, he made little headway. For four years he labored, spending all day at the mint and all evening puzzling over the inscriptions. Meanwhile, correspondents throughout India deluged him in his role of secretary of the Asiatic Society with coins and inscriptions that needed to be acknowledged, translated, and cataloged.

From one of them came the clue Prinsep lacked. In 1837 Captain Edward Smith visited the stupa at Sanchi and sent Prinsep copies of short inscriptions he found on the granite railings. They were in the same script as the pillar inscriptions, but had been laid out in separate lines, one on each railing. Prinsep guessed that they must record the names of individuals who had donated to the shrine. Each line

Towering 32 feet and weighing up to 50 tons, this highly polished column of sandstone surmounted with a seated lion was erected at Lauriya Nandangarh near the modern Nepalese border in the third century BC at the command of the Buddhist king Ashoka. Ashoka had his edicts and laws inscribed on such pillars, as well as on rocks and in caves, in order to instruct the people throughout his vast realm and unite the kingdom under one rule.

ended in the same characters, which Prinsep hazarded must mean gift, or given—in Sanskrit, *danam*. That insight allowed him to establish the characters for the letters *d*, *n*, and *m*, and those meager clues provided Prinsep with all the information he needed. Helped by a distinguished Brahmin scholar, or pandit, he set about deciphering the pillar inscription. It proved to be a religious edict urging rules of behavior similar to those of Buddhism, beginning "Thus spake King Devanampiya Piyadasi . . ."

But solving the puzzle of the script had only posed another mystery: Who Piyadasi was and when he lived remained frustratingly unclear. Among the Sanskrit historical texts of the Hindus, lists recorded the names of many early kings, but not that of Piyadasi. Meanwhile, another of Prinsep's regular correspondents, George Turnour, found a promising reference in Buddhist histories in Ceylon to a King Piyadasi, the first Ceylonese ruler to adopt the faith. But why should a king of that relatively small southern island be proclaiming his values throughout northern India?

A few weeks afterward, another work furnished Turnour with the answer. Piyadasi was not just the name of the Ceylonese king, but the epithet of an Indian ruler also known as Ashoka, who came to the throne 218 years after Buddha's Enlightenment. Ashoka's name did indeed appear in the Hindu texts as a member of the Mauryan dynasty, which ruled much of India for about 150 years, from around 325 BC. In Himalayan Buddhist sources the king was named as an early patron of the religion.

Prinsep's breakthrough would make Ashoka the best known of all Indian rulers who reigned before about AD 1100. But the effort of deciphering the script, which was named Ashoka Brahmi, had left the Englishman fatally weakened. Shortly afterward, while working on yet more inscriptions, he began to suffer headaches that heralded the onset of severe mental disorder. In 1838, his illness worsening, Prinsep sailed back to England where, aged 40, he died the next year without regaining his sanity.

Scholars now know of around 150 of Ashoka's inscriptions, carved onto the faces of rocks or on stone pillars, marking out a domain that stretched across the whole of northern India and south below the central plateau of the Deccan. Placed at strategic sites near borders, cities, and trade routes, the words of Ashoka made the king a presence in the lives of even those subjects far removed from his capital in Pataliputra, on the Ganges. And they provide the modern world with an unparalleled insight into the personality of one of India's earliest rulers.

Ashoka ascended the throne around 269 BC, inheriting the rich empire founded by his grandfather Chandragupta Maurya nearly half a century before. Eight years after becoming king, Ashoka converted to Buddhism in remorse at the loss of life involved in an earlier military campaign. Now the same edicts that announced this conversion urged his subjects to follow *dhamma*, or law, a code of morality that was based largely upon Buddhist tenets such as nonviolence to all living creatures, religious tolerance, and support of religious mendicants.

For the king, dhamma went beyond religion to include social welfare measures. The edicts told how Ashoka set up hospitals for animals as well as for humans, provided for plantings of medicinal herbs, and constructed roads flanked by shade trees and water wells for the comfort of travelers.

Commerce and industry thrived under Ashoka. Busy trade routes crossed rich farmland, and taxes poured into the coffers in Pataliputra. Megasthenes, the late-fourth-century-BC Greek ambassador whose writings would help Sir William Jones pinpoint the location of Pataliputra and establish a rough chronology of early India, marveled at this vast city, and understandably so. Modern estimates place its population in about 250 BC at more than 210,000; according to Megasthenes the city stretched for more than nine miles along the Ganges and was nearly two miles wide. This vast expanse was surrounded by a wooden palisade with 64 gates, within which stood parks with tame peacocks, fish ponds, and ornamental trees and shrubs. The royal palace, made of stone, was embellished with countless carvings and sculptures, and Megasthenes' successor, Aelian, was moved to compare the structure with similar establishments in great Persian cities of the day. At the palace of Pataliputra, he noted, was much that was "calculated to excite admiration, and with which neither Susa, with all its costly splendor, nor Ecbatana, with all its magnificence, can vie."

Because much of Pataliputra now lies buried beneath the silt of the Ganges Valley and the present-day city of Patna, the site poses special problems for archaeologists. But limited excavations earlier this century furnished tantalizing confirmation of ancient Greek descriptions. In the 1920s digging disclosed a section of a double row of upright timbers, 15 feet high and almost as far apart, that seemed

One of the oldest remaining records of what early Indian wooden architecture looked like, the entrance of the Lomas Rishi cave was hewn out of living rock in the third century BC. King Ashoka donated such chambers to various devout communities as a sign of his religious impartiality. Sometimes carved in imitation of the wooden structures used as temporary havens by wandering ascetics during the monsoon season, these rock caves offered more substantial shelter for monks and traders alike.

to extend indefinitely. Filled with earth, the wooden framework would have made a formidable defense similar to the palisade mentioned by Megasthenes.

Some dangers, however, were unstoppable. As early as 1912, archaeologists uncovered the remains of the great Mauryan palace and established that the building had been destroyed by fire sometime around the fourth century AD. In the remains of an imposing assembly hall, the heat of the flames had broken the 10-foot polished stone pillars that once bore the wooden roof; wooden platforms that supported the pillars were marked by circles of ashes on the floor. How many columns once stood in the hall is not clear—estimates range from 80 to 225—but their arrangement at regular 15-foot intervals seems to be modeled on similar examples in Persepolis, the capital of the mighty Achaemenid empire of Persia overrun by Alexander the Great. For centuries the Persians had influenced India's northwestern region around the city of Taxila: now it appeared that Ashoka had imported Persian ideas and, possibly, Persian masons in a conscious emulation of their mighty empire.

Among those who benefited from Ashoka's imperial designs were his fellow Buddhists, although the king was careful to stay on good terms with all the religions of his empire, which remained largely non-Buddhist. Legend has it that he built 84,000 stupas commemorating the events and relics of Buddha's life; he also held a great council to clarify Buddhist beliefs, confused after more than 200 years of oral tradition, and sent out monks to spread the religion throughout the subcontinent and the island of Ceylon.

Ashoka's missionaries would establish strongholds of the Buddhist faith from which it would eventually spread throughout Southeast Asia. The future of his empire, however, was not so secure. Following his death around 232 BC, the Mauryan dynasty endured only a few decades before the last of Chandragupta's heirs was assassinated, in about 185 BC. The empire fragmented and, once again, northern India was reduced to a shifting mosaic of independent states following Brahmanic beliefs.

If the glories of the Mauryans have largely vanished, the same could not be said for some of the most distinctive ancient monuments discovered by

Architectural motifs, most likely adapted from elements seen on Roman sarcophagi, are evident in this scene rendered in gold and rubies on a second-century-AD relic casket discovered in 1834 in Bimaran, Afghanistan. Buddha, his right hand raised in a gesture of reassurance, stands beneath a stylized archway similar in design to that of the entrance of the Lomas Rishi cave.

A FLEETING GLIMPSE OF BACTRIA'S GOLD-FILLED GLORY DAYS

No archaeologist can anticipate all the obstacles that might crop up in the course of a dig. And as the Uzbek archaeologist Victor Sarianidi learned in 1978, this is especially true when the excavation site lies in a country in the grip of a civil war. Sarianidi, a Bronze Age specialist, was the leader of a joint Soviet-Afghan expedition that made a surprising discovery while excavating at Tillya Tepe, the "golden hill," in northern Afghanistan: seven graves dug around AD 100, not long after nomads known as the Kushana established a powerful state to replace the Greco-Bactrian empire whose collapse they had caused.

Because ancient writings describe almost nothing of the formation of the Kushana empire, Sarianidi realized that the tombs' contents promised to cast light on what was then considered a dark age. And the burials—located as they were at a crossroads of the fabled Silk Road that once connected the Mediterranean world with the Orient—did not disappoint. Inside each one rested the remains of a lidless wood coffin, a skeleton, and a collection of gold plaques, jewelry, and other grave goods, including the delicate crown shown at right. Displaying Bactrian, Greco-Roman, Scythian, and Asian in-

A woman's skeleton lies in Tomb 6 at Tillya Tepe (above). Gold disks, earrings, and other jewelry lie among the bones, and a collapsible crown (right) graces her skull. Archaeologists speculate the headpiece was made so that its owner, perhaps a nomad princess, could stow it in her saddlebag for transport. In the photograph at upper right, workers excavate Tomb 1.

fluence, the artifacts offered compelling evidence that even at this early date, trade between East and West along the Silk Road was highly developed, and the sharing of ideas extensive.

Unfortunately, Sarianidi's find proved as ill-timed as it was dramatic. Only months before, revolutionaries replaced Afghanistan's military regime with a government that oppressed the Muslim majority, and violence spread across the countryside. "We were not caught in any

Evidence of contact between widely dispersed cultures, an Indian hump-backed ox, or zebu, adorns the translucent gemstone at left, which was found in Tomb 3 at Tillya Tepe. Similarly, the pendant below bears the image of Aphrodite, Roman goddess of love, but has been outfitted with Bactrian wings and an Indian forehead mark.

fighting," Sarianidi recalled, "but one morning armed tribesmen came on horseback, like sand devils off the desert, circling Tillya Tepe, asking angry questions. The frightened workmen implored us not to say anything, or we would be shot." The archaeologist accepted their counsel, and the horsemen took off.

The unrest did affect the amount of time the team had to unearth and document the artifacts—some 20,000 pieces in all. The weather had already become rainy and raw by mid November, and Sarianidi pondered calling off the dig. But then a worker stumbled across the first tomb, and much to Sarianidi's consternation, five more were found in short order. The seventh turned up in the last week of the expedition. "Simple arithmetic showed that we needed at least six weeks on the average to explore but one burial site, but we had only a week left to do everything," he wrote.

Faced with worsening weather and mounting unrest, Sarianidi ordered the final tomb covered up and armed guards posted. On February 8, 1979, he hurried off to Kabul, where he handed over his discoveries before leaving the country. In 1982 he received permission to photograph the treasures of Tillya Tepe, but continued fighting would prevent him from resuming excavation of the golden hill.

the early European investigators. The cave temples and monasteries carved deep into the living rock of the Western Ghats—the great escarpment behind the west-coast port of Bombay—required no excavation to reveal their grandeur. For the most part, these monuments stood much as they had been left by the communities of Buddhist monks who started building them around the start of the third century BC. The Buddhists chiseled out pillared halls, chapels, and stupas; in the viharas, cells were cut into the sides of rectangular halls, each with a rock bed, sometimes with a carved pillow.

The builders of some caves consciously incorporated elements of traditional wooden architecture. In a cave at Lomas Rishi, on Barabar Hill, for example, monks of the Ajivika sect carved an entrance with an imitation of the bamboo screens above the doorways of contemporary wooden buildings. In other caves, the carvers imitated wood-construction techniques by supporting the ceiling with stone pillars, as if it were a wooden roof.

Such grandiose structures—some of the western monasteries comprised several hundred separate caves—testify to the flourishing economy of the Andhra dynasty. Working from their base in the east central city of Amaravati, the Andhras—also known as the Satavahanas—had established during the first century BC a domain that eventually stretched from coast to coast across the high plateau of the central Deccan. The cave-carving monks depended on donations from wealthy urban merchants who were the traditional supporters of Buddhism: The rock inscriptions that record their donations even mention contributions from foreign traders, seafaring merchants from Arabia and Rome who visited ports such as Bharuch. For such men, the monasteries served a practical as well as a religious purpose. Often sited at the heads of passes on important trade routes, they provided shelter for traders making their laborious journeys through the mountains and a place for the exchange of reliable information.

The merchants of the Andhra empire helped finance other Buddhist monuments as well. Surely the greatest of these was the stupa discovered by British army colonel Colin Mackenzie, a student of Indian history and an avid collector of antiquities, when he visited the site of Amaravati in 1797. Mackenzie, who would later become surveyor general of India, had learned that building crews, while digging for construction materials at one of the many mounds scattered over the Amaravati area, had been turning up elaborately sculptured slabs of stone. When he went to investigate, he found that the mound was partly overgrown with jungle, but he could see that it had once been encased in bricks and stone slabs. Mackenzie had no doubt that he was standing on the remnants of a significant ancient monument.

His military duties kept Mackenzie from returning to Amaravati until 1816, when he descended on the mound with a team of assistants and draftsmen. He could not have been pleased with what he found: The stupa had been considerably diminished by the work of scavengers since he first saw it, and the landowner was digging a water tank into the top of the dome. Scarcely daunted, Mackenzie and his staff proceeded to conduct a survey of the jumbled ruins. At the same time, Mackenzie appropriated a number of the remaining carvings, which eventually found their way to museums in India and in England, where—with other Amaravati sculptures unearthed later—they would become the premier treasures of the Indian collection at the British Museum, surpassing any single assembly of ancient Indian sculpture outside the subcontinent itself. Several other archaeological expeditions to the stupa followed Mackenzie's pioneering venture, and by 1881 the mound had been reduced to nothing more than a large hole in the ground.

Mackenzie's studies and those of later investigators revealed that the so-called Great Stupa of Amaravati must rank as the most magnificent monument of ancient Indian Buddhism. The dome, estimated to have been about 140 feet in diameter, stood some 60 feet high. It rested on a circular platform, called a drum, standing about six feet tall and measuring more than 160 feet across. Surrounding the drum was an intricately carved, 10-foot stone railing broken at the north, south, east, and west by wide gateways.

Careful examination of the sculptures retrieved from Amaravati has revealed that the stupa was erected in stages over a period of several hundred years, beginning in about the third century BC. It probably reached its highest stage of development sometime around the end of the second century AD. Unfortunately, though, the haphazard nature of the early archaeology undertaken at the site has made it impossible for scholars to determine the original placement of the sculptures and other decorative carvings—many of which portray scenes from the life of Buddha *(pages 90-91)*. Most researchers, however, believe that these depictions appeared along the interior surface of the railing.

As at the caves carved laboriously out of living rock, numerous inscriptions found at the Great Stupa of Amaravati proclaim the

Two voluptuous yakshis *decorate this delicately carved, first-century-AD ivory plaque that originated in central India but was found to the north, in Begram, Afghanistan. The Andhra artisans of India were renowned for their ivory work, and one of their pieces turned up as far away as the Roman city of Pompeii.*

generous sponsorship of the Andhra mercantile class. And rich finds of a well-developed system of coinage confirm the success with which these merchants plied their trade. Tens of thousands of coins gathered during the first decades of the 19th century charted, in their symbols, portraits, and inscriptions, most of India's known history since about the beginning of the Christian era; a few others promised to tell an even older story, bearing dual inscriptions, one in a local language, the other in Greek. Others still, with only Greek characters adorning unmistakably classical portraits, appeared to be the work of the Greek kingdom of Bactria, where Alexander the Great had founded settlements in the late fourth century BC.

Bactria lay in what is now Afghanistan, and it was from the Afghan capital of Kabul that further details emerged in the 1830s. In 1832 Charles Masson—whose discovery of the ruins of Harappa six years before would later inspire Alexander Cunningham to examine the site—had heard of innumerable ancient coins to be found on the plain of Begram, 25 miles from Kabul. When he visited the plain in 1833, however, the local people proved reluctant to give up any of the rumored antiquities, until one old man eventually yielded a small, worthless coin. Masson bought it anyway, and once the Afghans saw that the stranger was willing to pay, more began to produce their treasures. By the time the winter snows came, Masson had amassed some 1,865 copper coins. Over the next three years he collected nearly 18,000 more. His biggest and final haul came in 1837, when, as he wrote later, "I had the plain well under control, and was able constantly to locate my people upon it." In that bumper-crop year, he noted, "I obtained 60,000 copper coins, a result with which I was well pleased."

Masson donated his vast coin collection to the grateful Asiatic Society and, together with Alexander Cunningham and the ailing James Prinsep, began trying to make sense of the story it told. Broadly ordered, the coins recorded centuries of declining Greek influence as the Bactrians, sometimes called Indo-Greeks, slowly absorbed Indian culture. During this process of assimilation, the regal Greek profiles and portraits of the hero Hercules on the early coins gave way to Buddhist and Hindu symbols, and to animals such as elephants, lions, and bulls.

The coins reflected the 400 years of instability in northern India following the downfall of the Mauryan empire, as the focus of Indian civilization shifted toward the northwestern Gandhara region around the Persian-influenced city of Taxila, in what is now northern Pakistan. Here, in the second century BC, successive waves of invaders led by the Bactrians swept down from Asia through the Hindu Kush mountains to the north, establishing brief domain before themselves falling to new conquerors. The Bactrians gave way early in the first century BC to the Scythians, a nomadic people from the Asian interior; the Scythians themselves were succeeded by the Parthians of Persia around the beginning of the Christian era or perhaps even earlier. During the first century AD, the Kushanas, a tribal people from Chinese central Asia, finally established an empire that reached its height under the rule of a king named Kanishka, a Buddhist convert who seems to have ascended to his throne in either AD 78 or 144.

The site of Taxila, standing amid the fertile plains and hills of the ancient Gandhara region, had been among Alexander Cunningham's early discoveries, but extensive excavation waited until the 20th century, when the city became the subject of digs led by two later directors of the Archaeological Survey: Sir John Marshall for nearly two decades starting in 1912 and Sir Mortimer Wheeler in the 1940s. What they discovered there were the remains of not one but three successive cities, erected within a couple of miles of each other.

The earliest city—called Taksashila after its founder—stood on a 60-foot-high hillock known as the Bhir mound. Taksashila had been occupied from around the sixth or fifth century BC to around the second century BC, when the Bactrian invaders founded nearby a new city called Sirkap, arranged along Greek lines. The third city, Sirsukh, which was built by the Kushanas in about the first century AD, remains relatively unexplored—waterlogged ground as well as modern villages on the site make excavation difficult.

On the Bhir mound, however, findings that included telltale Northern Black Polished Ware reflected the urbanization that had oc-

The vitality of King Kanishka, whose name means "most vigorously youthful," is asserted even in this headless sandstone statue from the late first to mid second century AD. The king is dressed in the apparel of his nomadic ancestors from Chinese central Asia. Though the king was a patron of Buddhism, he evidently carried out certain non-Buddhist practices and is seen on the gold coin at right conducting a Persian fire ritual.

curred in the Ganges Valley between the sixth and third centuries BC. And on one level, dating to the late fourth century BC, diggers found an earthenware vessel containing a vast hoard of coins, including three silver Greek didrachms that were probably evidence of Alexander the Great's brief stay at Taxila. By clearing an area near the center of the site, Marshall was able to gain a picture of the city, which he found singularly unimpressive. Taxila, he reported, had been a "rambling conglomeration of ill-aligned and ill-built walls of plastered rubble" lining narrow, twisting streets. For his part, Wheeler later noted that the place resembled "rather the slum of a poverty-stricken suburb than the central lay-out of a capital city."

Excavations at the later Parthian city of Sirkap revealed a more pleasant prospect. Within massive stone walls, white or color-washed stone buildings in yellows, blues, reds, and greens fit into a classic chessboard pattern with a north-south axis—which Marshall called Main Street—on which stood the royal palace. Walking along Main Street around AD 40, he speculated, one would pass small, single-story shops with here and there Buddhist, Jain, or Hindu temples, and shrines testifying to the city's standing as a religious center. The work of the Greek-influenced sculptors, masons, and artisans the Bactrians brought with them is evident in the architecture—just north of the city, for example, stood the Ionic, porticoed temple of Jandial, probably used for Persian fire worship. It is also apparent in finds of luxury items such as gold and jewelry, and in the hoards of coins and valuables buried for protection by the Parthians who occupied Sirkap when it was invaded by advancing Kushanas around the year AD 60.

By the time Kanishka mounted the Kushana throne, his empire stretched from central Asia, including parts of what are now Afghanistan and Pakistan, to the upper valley of the Ganges. The king's realm stood on bustling and profitable trade routes. To the north ran the great overland Silk Road linking China with the Roman Empire, and other major routes led south to northern India and to the western coast, where goods were shipped across the Arabian and Red Seas to the bustling Roman port of Alexandria in Egypt.

The reign of Kanishka was marked by peace and prosperity, and by political stability, religious tolerance, and patronage of the arts. In this nurturing environment, Indian art flowered. Carvings in particular were in great demand to supply the many temples and stupas established or enlarged by the Kushanas, and sculpture flourished

A monk by the name of Buddharakshita—
he who is protected by the Buddha—carries
an incense burner to a stupa in this first-
century-AD petroglyph in the mountains
of today's Pakistan. More than 20,000
inscriptions and petroglyphs were left here
by pilgrims, monks, and traders who journeyed along the ancient Silk Road.

in the two major artistic centers of Gandhara and Mathura. Although
most such works have been lost, stolen, damaged, or destroyed over
the centuries, much remains, and an intact trove occasionally comes
to light to further illuminate the craft of these ancient artisans.

In early 1985 the state government of Punjab, India, was mounting
an archaeological excavation in the village of Sanghol, at the ruins of
a Kushana stupa built between the first and second centuries AD. On
the chilly, sunny morning of February 1, the archaeologist at the site,
Yog Raj, was summoned by a laborer to come and see "a very beautiful brick" that he had uncovered a little more than a foot beneath
the path surrounding the stupa. When Raj went to the worker's
trench, what he found was in fact a finely carved pillar of red sand-

stone. He called his most experienced workmen to the trench, and after several hours of digging they revealed another pillar, then another. The same afternoon, Raj discovered a whole pile of carved stones, pillars, and beams stacked horizontally in a pit where they might have been placed under threat from attack: "I realized I had struck gold," he wrote later.

Along with its many other artifacts, the site yielded a total of 117 fine Mathuran sculptures, some in mint condition, from the railing that once surrounded the stupa. The fine-textured sandstone from which they were cut was softer and easier to carve than the stone that had been used for the great king Ashoka's pillars, and the sculptors of Sanghol exploited this workability to their advantage. They created lifelike scenes of surpassing beauty, where the *yakshis*—celestial females that traditionally adorned stupas—had become voluptuous, semiclad manifestations of eternal feminine beauty, spied on from balconies by mortal men and women. Landscapes of trees and rolling hills threw into the foreground delicate details such as water dripping into a swan's beak.

Such artistic achievement was matched by that of the Gandhara school in the northwest. Here, the fine carvings possess details more at home in Greece or Rome—togalike garments, Corinthian columns, Athenian sandals—providing unmistakable evidence of classical influence. Whether this impulse came from traditions established two centuries earlier by the Bactrian Greeks or from increasing contact with the Greco-Roman world in the first century is not clear. Certainly both influences were at work in the region, whose position at the crossroads of East and West had for centuries made it an active center of cultural exchange.

Around the opening of the Christian era, sculptors for the first time broke with a 500-year-old tradition and began portraying the figure of Buddha himself rather than representing him with divine symbols such as footprints, a bodhi tree, or empty thrones. Indeed, the carvers at Gandhara mass-produced statues of the Buddha. And among King Kanishka's coins, along with those showing deities from Rome, Alexandria, and central Asia, as well as Hindu gods such as Shiva and Skanda-Kumara, is one on which a figure of Buddha, identified by a Greek inscription, appears on the reverse of an image of the king himself worshiping at a Persian fire altar.

The origins of this sudden development are unclear, but it is plain that by around the end of the first century AD both Buddhism and Hinduism were changing. The representation of Shiva on coins was a sign of the spread of *bhakti*, the devotional worship of deities. Bhakti marked a shift away from patronage of the ancient Vedic sacrifice and a movement toward worship of two insignificant Vedic gods—Vishnu and Shiva—who slowly increased in importance.

As for Buddhism, Kanishka himself sponsored a great council to stabilize the faith, and a new strain emerged in which believers were helped to achieve Nirvana—previously the exclusive goal of monks—by saintly beings called Bodhisattvas. Buddha, long revered as an exceptional human being, became worshiped as a savior and god. This devotional faith, scholars argue, required its own icon, and the stone carvers of Gandhara drew on the region's heritage of depicting deities in human form. Icons of Buddha soon spread throughout India: By the late second century AD, they adorned even the Great Stupa of Amaravati, home of the southern Andhra dynasty.

In its diverse origins, Gandharan art is a fitting symbol of first-century north India, which stood at the hub of a trade network linking India, China, and central Asia with the Greco-Roman world around the Mediterranean Sea. In addition to the overland Silk Road and its offshoots that connected the peninsula with much of Asia, a sea route linked the Indus delta with the Persian Gulf. Meanwhile, Roman ships plied the Red Sea route, taking advantage of the mastery of the seasonal monsoon winds about the middle of the first century to make speedy crossings from the Indian west-coast ports to the city of Alexandria.

Roman seafarers also ventured around the tip of the Indian peninsula, and it was on the eastern coast that dramatic evidence of their presence first came to light in 1944, when Sir Mortimer Wheeler visited the port city of Madras. Exploring the city museum on a hot May day when a Japanese bombing raid had caused a general evacuation of the area, he found himself alone to wander as he wished. Rooting around in a cupboard, Wheeler discovered the unmistakable remains of a long-necked, two-handled amphora, a container used in the Mediterranean to transport wine and oil. Excited inquiries led him farther down the coast to the town of Pondicherry; there, in a dust-covered library cabinet, he found sherds of a pottery he recognized at once as Arrentine ware, named for the central Italian town of Arezzo where it originated.

The following summer, Wheeler moved his team south from Taxila to the coastal village of Arikamedu, a couple of miles from

Pondicherry. There, after 12 days of digging in the wet sand and silt, one of his workers turned up a Roman pot sherd that, miraculously, bore its maker's stamp—VIBII, or VIBIE. Investigation showed that the mark identified the Vebia family, which turned out ceramic ware in Arezzo for about 150 years, from the early first century BC. That Arikamedu had once been an Indo-Roman trading center was further indicated by the discovery of the remains of a massive warehouse and two large tanks that were probably used for producing and dyeing Indian muslin for export.

Goods from India were highly prized by wealthy Romans, and Rome-bound trading vessels carried ivory, perfumes, spices, and valuable woods, as well as more exotic cargoes of elephants and rhinoceroses, and fashionable prostitutes and slaves. In return, India imported Roman wines, musical instruments, glass, girls for the harems of the wealthy—and gold coins, which have turned up throughout India. Indeed, during the first century, so much Roman gold found its way to India that some Romans feared that the drain might weaken the imperial economy.

Splendid ruins of a Buddhist monastery built upon a rocky precipice some 2,000 years ago rise above the plains outside the modern town of Takht-i-Bahi in Pakistan. Thirty chapels were built around the main stupa and, at one time, each chamber held a life-size statue of the Buddha.

To satisfy Rome's insatiable appetites, Indian traders turned to Southeast Asia. As early as the fifth century BC, hardy sailors had braved the Bay of Bengal to search for gold and tin in Sri Lanka and beyond in the Malay Peninsula and Burma. Now their quest was for spices: The tiny islands of the Moluccas in Indonesia, for example, were the ancient world's only source of cloves, the unopened buds of a tree found nowhere else. The spice trade took Indian seafarers from the subcontinent around Southeast Asia, where they established trading posts and spread their religion and culture as they went: In what are now Cambodia and Vietnam, second-century Indian settlers and converts to Hinduism raised mighty temples to Shiva; by around the fourth century, Sanskrit would be established as the region's official language.

Among India's gifts to her eastern neighbors, Buddhism also ranked high. By sea, descendants of Ashoka's missionaries to Sri Lanka would carry it across the Bay of Bengal to Burma and Thailand, and then farther still to Sumatra, Cambodia, Vietnam, and Borneo. From the northern empire of Kanishka, the faith traveled overland along the Silk Road through central Asia to China, from where it spread to Korea and, in the sixth century, to Japan.

In its homeland, however, Buddhism was already in decline. When the Kushanas were overthrown by Sassanian invaders from Iran around the middle of the third century, the center of power switched from Gandhara back to the east. It was from the ancient heartlands of Magadha, in the lower Ganges Valley, that India's next great dynasty would arise, motivated by a resurgent Hinduism that would gradually assimilate much of the weakened Buddhist faith during the following centuries.

TEMPLES OF LIVING ROCK

When they set out for India in 1785, the British artists Thomas and William Daniell, an uncle and nephew team, knew practically nothing of the wonders awaiting them. In this monument-crowded land some of the most awesome works of the past lay near Bombay, primarily in the mountains west of the city. At Kanheri, Karli, Ellora, and Elephanta, cave temples had long served the religious needs of Hindus, Buddhists, and Jains alike. Some were natural caverns that had been embellished with timbered roofs and wooden adornments, but the majority had been carved by hand deep into the living rock by hundreds, if not thousands, of stoneworkers.

Scholars studying unfinished cave temples at Kanheri and elsewhere have learned that they were cut from the ceiling down, with narrow tunnels facilitating the initial work of enlargement. The finished temples and shrines were so adroitly executed—with enormous chambers, sculpted walls, and elaborate columns—that it is hard to believe they are part of the rock and not separate from it.

Traveling in India for several years, the Daniells reached Bombay in 1793 and there met up with the English painter James Wales, who was making an extensive survey of the temples *(above)*. Wales guided the Daniells to the caves, and the three set about recording what they saw. Arriving back in England a year later, the Daniells published both the fruits of their own labors and those of Wales, who meanwhile had died—supposedly from the putrid air he had breathed in the caves. To make prints from the watercolor sketches, the Daniells used a new medium called aquatint. Similar to etching, this process permitted the printing of various black and gray tones, with additional colors touched in by hand. The public responded enthusiastically to the aquatints, prompting other artists to head for India. A sampling of images by the Daniells and those who followed them forms the basis of this essay.

A panorama of the basalt escarpment at Ellora (above) affords a glimpse of the rock-cut shrines found there. At the center rises the Hindu temple of Kailasa, one of two freestanding sanctuaries carved from the cliff. Also visible are some of the 34 other shrines tunneled into the rock. Of the total, 12 are Buddhist, 17 Hindu, and five Jain. The original watercolor sketches were made during the monsoon season when waterfalls cascaded over the ridges.

Considered a masterpiece of freestanding rock-cut architecture, the Kailasa Hindu Temple complex (above) *at Ellora sits in the pit of stone from which it was carved in the mid eighth century AD. The farthest building, the sanctuary, rises 107 feet, and at middle left is the shrine that houses Shiva's sacred bull, Nandi. Their*

The facade of the Buddhist worship hall at Karli shows the rich decorative detail typical of Indian rock-cut temples. Four lions adorn the bell-shaped capital of the column to the left. The square building on the right is a later addition and houses an early-18th-century Hindu shrine. The interior of the main hall is visible through the vaulted window. An inscription at the base of the window, recording the grant of a village to the Karli monks, helps to confirm the date of the sanctuary as the first century AD, when the cave was carved within a 10-to-15-year period.

Two rows of pillars line the horseshoe-shaped hall of the Karli Buddhist Temple (above), largest and finest of the rock-cut caves in the Deccan. It is some 45 feet wide and 123 feet deep. Embracing lovers on kneeling elephants top the columns, which rise from pot-shaped bases. The columns lead to the massive hemisphere of solid rock, a stupa. Above it, sacred patterns embellish the underside of an original wooden umbrella. The barrel-vaulted ceiling, soaring 46 feet, is arched

Dominating the dramatic south-central chapel within the rock-cut Hindu temple on Elephanta Island is an 18-foot-tall, three-headed sculpture of Shiva symbolizing the god's aspects as cosmic creator, preserver, and destroyer. The figures on the pillars and in the wall panels depict events and manifestations of Shiva. To enter this sixth-century-AD temple, positioned some 250 feet above the waters of Bombay's harbor, worshipers had to ascend a steep stairway cut from the cliff.

THE GOLDEN AGE OF THE GUPTAS

In this detail from one of numerous murals in Ajanta's 29 rock-hewn caves, Prince Mahajanaka bids his mother farewell as a female fly-whisk bearer stands behind him. Most paintings were done during a 20-year period in the fifth century AD, part of India's Golden Age.

The original quarry was tigers, but what the hunters would find that April day in 1819 would be infinitely more exotic. The tiger hunters, all cavalry officers of the British Raj and headquartered at Madras, were on maneuvers in the Sahyadri Hills when they decided to spend some free time pursuing the great cats near the village of Ajanta. The area was known for its game animals, but forays there were dangerous. Ajanta was the territory of primitive Bhil tribesmen, said to be no less fierce than the tigers themselves, and no more welcoming to strangers.

Nevertheless, the hunters set out, hiking along a riverbed, their uniform jackets splotches of scarlet in the greens and browns of the thorn scrub and dry forest. Following a native child who promised to lead them to a ravine rich in tiger lairs, the soldiers finally arrived at a promontory overlooking a large, horseshoe-shaped gorge. The site did, indeed, look promising: The ravine floor was alive with wild vegetation that crept and twined up the walls of the curving cliff side. There, surely, were havens aplenty for tigers, and the soldiers started toward it.

As they neared their destination, one of the hunters pushed aside some branches, and suddenly, all thoughts of tigers were forgotten. Staring down at the Englishmen was a huge Buddha, hewn out of the cliff's rock, his hands gesturing a mute benediction toward

his astonished visitors. The hunters could also see by now that the cliff was not the featureless monolith that it had appeared to be from the promontory. There was a doorway visible near the Buddha, a darkened portal carved deep into the cliff itself. They entered it, their human footsteps an alien accent among the tracks of tigers, bears, and monkeys.

What the soldiers had stumbled on would in time emerge as one of the greatest art troves of all antiquity, the last grand monument of what many scholars would call India's golden age. The tiger hunters had found the caves of Ajanta, lost to civilization for more than a thousand years.

The wonders of Ajanta consist of no fewer than 29 caves carved into the U-shaped bay of the cliff, comprising Buddhist temples and monasteries. These are adorned by some fine sculptures that, however valuable, pale into relative insignificance beside the priceless, uniquely preserved paintings that are Ajanta's greatest treasure—the still-vibrant murals covering almost all the walls of the vast shrine. The first stonecutters had begun chipping away at Ajanta's cliff in the second century BC, but the last burst of creative work at the site did not take place

At left, colonnaded entrances to Ajanta's caves line the steep basalt cliff looming over a bank of the Waghora River. Except for those numbered 9, 10, 19, 26, and 29 below, which were chaitya halls, or houses of worship, all the caves were monasteries featuring a large, square, covered central courtyard whose three inner sides were lined with as many as 25 small cells for the monks.

122

until some 700 years later, toward the end of the fifth century AD.

At that time, India was nearing the close of its golden age, the classical period that saw indigenous cultures and foreign strains coalesce and become refined in a matchless flowering of art, literature, science, and religion. The result was a culture at once highly sophisticated and intensely spiritual—one that, while purely Indian, would extend its influence well beyond the Indian subcontinent, leaving a legacy that lasts to this day.

This cultural flowering coincided with—and largely resulted from—a period of unusual political stability. After a time of fragmentation and foreign incursions, almost all of northern India was, by the fourth century AD, united under the imperial Guptas, whose dynastic name became synonymous with the golden age. The Guptas produced successively three monarchs of extraordinary caliber and two more of unusual competence before lesser scions of the line failed to hold the empire together in the face of internal factionalism and renewed foreign invasion. In all, the reigns of these five Gupta emperors lasted only about one hundred and fifty years, which is a remarkably short time when measured against the great achievements it encompassed. Indeed, so outstanding and pervasive was

Below, multipetaled flowers, fruit clusters, and a prancing pink elephant decorate the ceiling of Cave 1, a monastery sponsored by the great Vakataka emperor Harishena. The dull emerald pigment used to paint the meander at center was probably made from a mineral found in the basalt cliffs out of which the cave was gouged, while the yellows, oranges, reds, and browns came from ocher in the local clay.

Gupta cultural influence that some historians mark the end of their age as late as 600 or even 700 AD.

Yet even as the Guptas waned in the north, southward in the Deccan the Vakataka empire continued briefly to flourish. Vakataka kings had brought most of south India under their sway, just as the Guptas had done in the north. The two dynasties, though sometimes rivals, were also interrelated through marriage, and under Vakataka sovereignty the Gupta legacy was, for a time, expanded and carried forward. In fact, the caves of Ajanta, though their art showed Gupta influence, lay within Vakataka territory, and it was through Vakataka patronage that their great beauty was created.

In 1991 and 1992 Bombay photographer Benoy K. Behl sparked renewed interest in the murals of Ajanta by taking pictures of them in the near-total darkness of the caves. Forbidden to use flash equipment out of concern that the light might damage the paintings, Behl lengthened his exposure times to as much as 20 minutes. The resulting images, one of which is at right, proved so revealing scholars could make out details overlooked before, including retouching that had been done in the 10th century AD.

In its ponderous way, the British Empire was slow to realize what a cultural jewel it had stumbled across in Ajanta. For about two and a half decades after their discovery, the caves attracted from the West only limited scholarly interest and a few tourists. Then, in 1843, the great British architectural historian James Fergusson visited the site and subsequently complained to the East India Company, overlord of the area, that Ajanta was suffering from exposure, both to the weather and to souvenir hunters. In response, the company dispatched to Ajanta Captain Robert Gill, an artist attached to the Madras army. The captain was to copy as much as he could of the caves' marvelous murals.

Gill arrived at the site in 1844 and launched himself into his herculean labor. He copied the murals on canvas and made tracings and colored drawings of them. Eschewing a bungalow in a nearby village, he lived in the caves themselves, enchanted by them, obsessed with them, reveling in the long-abandoned splendor of a lost millennium. He married a beautiful Indian woman, and at night she would dance for him by firelight. On those evenings Gill mused, perhaps, on how the dance seemed a reflection of the murals themselves, their scenes depicting with such vitality the spirituality and sensuality so eternally intertwined in Indian thought and art: scenes of court life with handsome rajas and their lovely women, voluptuous and bejeweled; scenes of musicians and dancers, of woodlands and fragrant garlands, of frolicking demigods and beasts. And in the midst of it all, Buddhas and saintly Bodhisattvas, youthful and full of grace, surrounded by the pleasures of the world and yet beyond them all, transcendent and serene.

But Hindu legend has it that a curse lies over Ajanta. The story goes that Indra, a king of gods, once allowed his fellow deities a night of revelry on earth, provided they returned to heaven before dawn. So absorbed were they in their merriment, however, that the gods and goddesses failed to heed the rooster's crow. As punishment they were turned into pictures on Buddhist Ajanta's walls, frozen there for all time—immobile, but gods nonetheless, and quick to retaliate against mortals who presumed to defile or reproduce them. The shadow of their curse, it seemed, fell over Robert Gill.

Surviving dysentery, a broken leg, and political upheavals, Gill worked constantly for almost 20 years, copying the murals and dispatching successive batches of his paintings to London via Bombay. Finally, with almost all the important cave paintings reproduced, Gill's work was assembled in London's Crystal Palace for exhibition. But in 1866 fire destroyed the Palace, and along with it all but three or four of Gill's canvases. The tragedy almost destroyed the artist as well. Somehow he started over, but after about five years he fell terminally ill. Twenty-seven years after arriving at Ajanta, he died. He was buried just north of the caves.

In the 1870s a team from the Bombay School of Arts spent four seasons making new facsimiles—some of them as large as 30 feet square—which were again shipped to London. They were stored in the annex of the Victoria and Albert Museum. There was another fire, one that destroyed nothing of value in the annex except the Ajanta paintings. In succeeding years, more attempts were made to record the art of Ajanta and—with mixed results—to restore it. Much has been lost over time—whether from weather, greed, ineptitude, bad luck, or divine retribution—but preservation efforts continue to the present day.

Despite all the ill fortune that surrounded Ajanta, some excellent preservation work by Italian experts in the 1920s resulted in the publication of photographs of the cave paintings. And suddenly, more than a century after their discovery, the murals burst onto Western cultural consciousness. Britain's *Burlington Magazine* declared the paintings to be "perhaps the greatest artistic wonder of Asia," and in 1923, renowned ballerina Anna Pavlova performed an "Ajanta Ballet" at Covent Garden in London, her movements based on gestures of the figures in the paintings. Ancient Indian art had acquired 20th-century European chic.

A much deteriorated mural in Cave 2 (above) *demonstrates the combined effects of humidity-loving fungi and burrowing silverfish, beetles, and cockroaches. Both the microbes and insects feed on the organic ingredients of the plaster that covers the walls. After cultivating samples from this and other Ajanta caves, Indian researchers* (right) *were able to identify no fewer than 40 species of invading fungi in their efforts to stem further damage.*

However appreciative the Western aesthetes had at last become of the marvels of India's classical art, they probably were largely ignorant of the social and political factors that had produced it. Ancient Indians left little in the way of formal written histories, and it has been only in the last 200 years or so that linguists, archaeologists, and other specialists have sought to piece together a chronicle of the period. The primary evidence they have relied on comes from inscriptions on temple walls, on copper-plate land grants, and on the monumental pillars that dot India here and there; from the devices and inscriptions on ancient coins; and from the surviving secular and religious literature of the time, the accounts of Chinese monks who visited India, and archaeological remains.

In the last category, the remnants in northern India are comparatively scant: A major factor in the fall of the Gupta dynasty was successive invasions, beginning toward the end of the fifth century, by the Hunas, or White Huns—perhaps a branch of those same

Huns who, under Attila, were wreaking havoc in Europe at the time. Then in the 11th century came the fiercely iconoclastic Muslims, many of whom had no patience whatever with what they viewed as the blasphemous works of heathen idol worshipers. In those two invasions, much Gupta and Vakataka architecture perished, and with it its irreplaceable sculpture.

Given the intricate task of putting together the piecemeal evidence from remaining sources, it is not surprising that there are gaps in the chronicle of this classical period and controversies among scholars over certain facts. Much more is still being learned and remains to be investigated. Nevertheless, a fairly complete outline of the times is in place.

The exact origins of the Guptas are somewhat shadowy; indeed, while the word *gupta* can be translated as "protect" or "preserve," it can also mean "hidden." But historians agree on the basis of inscriptions that the patriarch of the family was a maharaja of the Brahmin class named Gupta, who lived sometime around AD 300. Gupta himself was not a major monarch, but he was an important landowner whose fiefdom ran along the borders of modern Bihar and Bengal. His son was one Ghatotkacha, another maharaja, whose importance to history rests mainly with the fact that he was the father of Chandragupta I, the founder of the Gupta empire and the first of its great rulers.

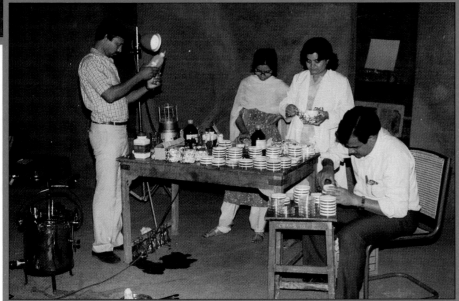

Some scholars believe that Chandragupta I—who could claim no kinship with the earlier Chandragupta Maurya, whose empire had flourished in India centuries before—began as no more than a local chieftain, like his father and grandfather, or perhaps as a talented and ambitious young soldier. But he took a direct and time-honored route to power: He married well. In AD 305 he wed Kumaradevi, a princess of the illustrious Licchavi dynasty, which ruled Magadha, a large territory in northern Bihar near Nepal. Ghatotkacha, who probably had imperial ambitions for his family, arranged the match. Some experts speculate that by joining Magadha to the Gupta holdings he meant to offset the growing power in the south of the Vakatakas and their allies. In any case, on ascending the throne around AD 319 or 320 after the death of his father, Chandragupta I assumed the imperial title of *maharajadhiraja*—king of kings. His capital at the time was probably at Prayag (modern Allahabad), though some historians contend that the governmental seat was at Pataliputra (Patna).

Although the details of his conquests are sketchy, Chandragupta I apparently did fairly well by his lofty title: By the time of his death in 335 the Guptas held sway over the whole central Ganges basin, a territory that today comprises modern Bihar and eastern Uttar Pradesh. But it was under Chandragupta's son and successor, Samudragupta, that the dynasty achieved true imperial status.

As a conqueror, Samudragupta was preeminent among the Gupta emperors and was greatly admired by the 19th-century European scholars whose studies first revealed the existence of his empire. The Britisher Vincent A. Smith, for one, hailed the Gupta ruler as the "Indian Napoleon," and mused that he was "endowed with no ordinary powers."

Details of Samudragupta's career as a soldier, statesman, philanthropist, and poet are comparatively abundant, largely because Harishena, his court poet and minister of peace and war, wrote them down for inscription on the so-called Allahabad pillar. This 40-odd-foot stone pillar, originally erected by the great Mauryan emperor Ashoka, stood first at Kaushambi, the site of Samudragupta's first major military battle, one in which he defeated three Naga kings. The pillar would be moved to Allahabad centuries afterward by the Mogul emperor Akbar.

In very polished Sanskrit verse and prose, the pillar inscription relates that Samudragupta was "dexterous in waging hundreds of various kinds of battles with only the strength of his prowess of arms. The beauty of his charming body was enhanced by the multiplicity of the confused wounds, caused by the blows of battle axes, arrows, spears, pikes, barbed darts, swords, lances, javelins, iron arrows, and many other weapons."

A number of coins were minted during Samudragupta's rule, and they have provided historians with considerable information about the Indian monarch. The first hoard of Gupta coins was discovered near Calcutta in 1783, but it was not until the 1830s that scholars succeeded in deciphering their inscriptions, which proved to

Images struck on the 1,600-year-old gold coins above portray Samudragupta, the second great Gupta emperor, as a powerful conqueror and benign music lover. At top, a long pennant flutters above a horse to be sacrificed in commemoration of Samudragupta's many victories, while at bottom, the seated, haloed monarch strums a sitarlike instrument called a vina.

be no less rapturous than the Allahabad pillar in extolling the emperor's multifaceted splendor. For example, the standard gold coin of his realm describes the ruler as "the unconquered one, whose victory was spread in hundreds of battles, having conquered his enemies, conquers heaven."

When it moves from elaborate praise to specifics, the Allahabad inscription tells that Samudragupta "violently uprooted" nine kings of northern India and annexed their kingdoms and that he commanded homage from a number of other kingdoms and republics along his frontier. Moving southward into the eastern Deccan—Vakataka territory—he led a successful foray as far as Kanchi (modern Conjeeveram), but he chose after this campaign merely to exact tribute from the rulers he had conquered and reinstate them.

Samudragupta's apparent aim was to establish a tightly knit realm along the lines of the Mauryan empire some five centuries earlier, and perhaps he recognized the pitfalls inherent in trying to govern directly too diffuse a territory. In any case, by the time his battles and diplomacies were over, Samudragupta's vast power extended from Assam to the borders of the Punjab, and he maintained diplomatic relations with Sri Lanka and other far-off islands.

Having thus established a *pax Gupta*, this most formidable of warriors spent the last quarter century of his life demonstrating that he was not solely a great general, but also a humanitarian, an intellectual, an artist and a patron of the arts, and a staunch and learned defender of the faith.

"With the support and approach of the miserable, poor, destitute and afflicted, his mind was ever engaged for their amelioration," says the Allahabad pillar, going on to relate how Samudragupta was also merciful to kings he had conquered, doing all he could to restore their fortunes. As to the emperor's artistic gifts, the pillar declares that "by virtue of his various exquisite poems, he reigned supreme as the king of poets among the learned people whose mainstay was poetry," and that the great legendary musicians "paled into insignificance by his sharp and cultured intellect and musical talent." Nothing remains by which modern critics might appraise the emperor's verse, but apparently Samudragupta himself was proud of his musical gifts. One of his coins depicts him playing a vina, a stringed instrument similar to a sitar.

Samudragupta, and most of the other Gupta emperors, were Vaishnavas—followers of the Hindu god Vishnu. The Allahabad in-

THE LOFTY DWELLING PLACE OF A SRI LANKAN MASTER BUILDER

Of the several capitals of the ancient island domain of Sri Lanka, the most intriguing by far is Sigiriya, built between AD 477 and 495 by Kasyapa I. Though the eldest son of the ruler Dhatusena I, Kasyapa was not born to a woman of royal blood, and thus he feared that his younger half-brother, the queen's offspring, might challenge his claim to the throne. So in AD 477, he chained his father to a rampart and entombed him alive, an act that sent his sibling fleeing into exile.

Kasyapa moved the capital 40 miles southeast, from its original site of Anuradhapura to Sigiriya, a massive rock outcrop that looms on the horizon and resembles a crouching lion. There, atop a cave-pocked promontory, some 650 feet high, which had served for centuries as a Buddhist monastic settlement, he built palaces and gardens. Below and to the west, he laid out a moat-ringed water garden. And

to the south, he dug a lake to capture water from the seasonal rains, which underground pipes carried to the gardens in dry months. The result was hardly the bastion of a beleaguered king, but a pleasure-filled estate on the grandest scale.

Scholars suspect that either Kasyapa died, spurring his brother to return, or that his exiled brother came back to Sri Lanka and captured the throne before the retreat could be finished.

No longer a capital, Sigiriya became a Buddhist monastery once again, and sometime after the 13th century it disappeared from the history books, only to be rediscovered by antiquarians in the 1800s. UNESCO-sponsored archaeologists and conservators have been at work at this extraordinary site since 1982.

To the west of Sigiriya, an arrow-straight pathway bisects three pleasure gardens. The first, located at the bottom of the picture, features a square island that was once surrounded by four L-shaped pools. The second, adjoining the first, has fountains that are fed by underground conduits and burble in rainy weather even today. A boulder to the left of the path borders the final garden, which a wall separates from the rising ground at the foot of the rock.

In the foreground, bottom left, visitors assemble near the remains of the Lion Gate, which, according to ancient chronicles, was the sole entryway to Sigiriya's terraced summit. Constructed in the shape of a lion, the gate admitted guests between two colossal paws and into the beast's mouth, where stairs, visible to the left of the gate, led to Kasyapa's brick and timber palace.

Below, pairs of celestial maidens painted more than 300 feet above ground carry flowers and gesture to one another. They form part of what an observer called a "gigantic picture gallery"—a 460-foot-long procession of beauties that stretched all along the western face of the rock. Today only this fragment and an adjacent patch survive, along with some traces of plaster and pigment elsewhere.

scription declares that Samudragupta was a "supporter of the real truth of scriptures," well versed in doctrine and dedicated to ruling by his religious precepts and traditions. Some of his coins featured Lakshmi, the consort of Vishnu, on one side, and he adopted the Garuda, the bird that bears Vishnu, as his insignia. It is also clear from one of the coins that, on completing his conquests, he performed the *ashvamedha*, or horse sacrifice, reviving an ancient Vedic rite of kingship that had fallen into disuse. His personal piety notwithstanding, Samudragupta—and all the other Gupta emperors—practiced religious tolerance. He respected all the Hindu cults, as well as Jainism, and he seemed to have a particular soft spot for Buddhism. He showed great hospitality to a noted Buddhist scholar, Vasubandhu, and he granted a request from the king of Sri Lanka for the building of a Buddhist monastery at Bodh Gaya.

Quasi-divine beings known as gandharvas *play a vina and cymbals in this frieze, which adorned a fifth-century temple at Nachna, in central India. Half-human, half-bird musicians of the gods, gandharvas are believed to shower good fortune upon those they favor.*

In sum, during a rule that lasted more than 40 years, Samudragupta seems to have been, in the words of the Allahabad inscription, "an embodiment of all virtues" who "remains an idol for meditation of those who can understand his merit and intellect." Indeed, he is regarded by some scholars as the greatest emperor of his illustrious line. Even so, after his death sometime around 375 there seems to have been a slight stutter-step in the ongoing Gupta march. This came in the person of Samudragupta's eldest son, Ramagupta, who proved in his brief rule that as a monarch and a man he was far below the dynastic standard.

For years Ramagupta's very existence was inferred only from his role as a protagonist in the political drama *Devichandraguptam*, by the playwright Vishakhadatta, a work that has not survived, but is referred to in other literature. Most experts chalked off Ramagupta as a fictional character. But the discovery in the 1940s of some copper coins bearing his name and the further find in 1969 near Vidisha of three Jain sculptures inscribed *Maharajadhiraja Ramagupta* attest to his historical reality.

According to the play, King Ramagupta led a magnificent army against a rebellious Scythian chieftain but was defeated by him. Besieged in a hill fort, Ramagupta ignominiously agreed to terms of surrender that involved giving up his beautiful queen, Dhruvadevi, to the Scythian victor. The queen, much offended by this arrangement, sought help from Ramagupta's younger brother, the soon-to-be-emperor Chandragupta II, who was then serving in Ramagupta's army. The brave and resourceful Chandragupta, along with several hundred young comrades, dressed up as women and thus gained entry into the enemy camp, where they killed the presumptuous Scythian chieftain. As emperor, Chandragupta II would finally defeat the Scythians altogether, driving out a hated foreign influence from northern India, and he would make his capital at Ujjain, the former Scythian stronghold.

Images of cavorting men, women, and boys decorate the center of this silver plate, one of the few surviving Gupta luxury items and a rare example of Gupta art from northwest India. Gold and silver items such as this were most likely used by kings and emperors.

Ramagupta's ultimate fate is unknown, although it was probably not pleasant. In any case, Chandragupta II, who married Dhruvadevi himself, took the throne in about 376, assuming the title Vikramaditya—"one who is like the sun in valor." As a conqueror and as a diplomat, Chandragupta II was a most worthy successor to his father, for it was under his reign that the borders of the Gupta empire stretched to their widest extent, across northern India from sea to sea, from the foothills of the Himalayas in the north and southward into the Deccan.

Chandragupta II was no doubt a competent general, but possibly of more importance to his dynasty's territorial ambitions was that, like his great-grandfather Ghatotkacha before him, he was mindful of the political importance of a propitious marriage. Thus Chandragupta II arranged to have his daughter Prabhavati wed Rudrasena II, king of the Vakatakas, who ruled over vast holdings in the Deccan. Rudrasena died young, leaving his Gupta widow the regent for their sons—and leaving Chandragupta II with a major influence over affairs in India's huge central plateau. Thus by a matrimonial coup the Gupta emperor effected an alliance between two great dynasties that theretofore had been, at best, uneasy neighbors.

Far more significant than its territorial extent, the rule of Chandragupta II is remembered as the high-water mark of classical Indian culture, a period of peace, prosperity, and intellectual achievement so glittering as to win a place in history alongside Periclean Athens, Augustan Rome, and Elizabethan England.

An important account of the empire under Chandragupta II survives in the memoir of a foreign observer, the Chinese Buddhist monk Fa Hsien, who spent about 10 years traveling in India to collect authentic copies of Buddhist scriptures. He was very impressed by what he saw. The "Middle Kingdom," as he called it, was a place of "temperate climate, without frost or snow; and the people are prosperous and happy without registration or official restrictions."

According to Fa Hsien, whose recollections were first translated by French scholars in the mid 1800s, the citizens of the Gupta empire enjoyed more liberties, including the freedoms of speech, expression, and movement, than did the people of China. "Those who want to go away, may go; those who want to stay, may stay," the monk reported, adding that this privilege even applied to foreigners.

Taxes were low, he noted, crime was rare, and punishment light. "The king in his administration uses no corporal punishments," he wrote; "criminals are merely fined according to the gravity of their offenses. Even for a second attempt at rebellion the punishment is only the loss of the right hand."

Even the disadvantaged were cared for in this prosperous land, Fa Hsien wrote. In the cities there were "free hospitals, and hither come all poor helpless patients, orphans, widowers, and cripples. They are well taken care of, a doctor attends them, food and medicine are being supplied according to their needs. They are all made quite comfortable and when they are cured, they go away."

On the whole, the monk described an almost utopian land of good government, charitable impulse, and temperate behavior. Hardly anyone ate meat or drank wine, Fa Hsien declared, and "no one kills any living thing."

More interested in piety than in politics, Fa Hsien never mentioned Chandragupta II by name, nor did he dwell on many particulars of imperial administration. Moreover, the monk seems to have had a tourist's bent for romanticizing his surroundings somewhat; for while Gupta India was by all accounts an extraordinarily blessed kingdom, it was not quite the pious paradise that Fa Hsien described. Plenty of Indians were not vegetarians, for example, and plenty of them, especially among the upper classes, were apparently also quite familiar with intoxicating liquor and other pleasures of the flesh.

The satirical literature of the day paints opulent and sensual pictures of Persian horses drawing fine carriages that carried handsome princes to the luxurious homes of beautiful courtesans. There are descriptions of streets lined with shops full of incense, perfumes, flowers, and ornaments, and there are also accounts of gambling halls, bordellos, and taverns.

Of course, the king himself lived particularly well. According to one satirical source, he awoke early in the morning to strains of music, donned magnificent clothes and jewels, then betook himself to an audience hall to receive important guests and hand out gifts and awards while his minions set up a bar in the garden. "The king and his companions drank wine out of ruby cups," the text relates, while "lutes were strummed; there was dance and music. In the evening the king returned to his palace and attended musical performances and dramatic shows in which women alone participated."

In the matter of women, the monarch's evening agenda probably also included attentions to one of his various wives, for polygamy was the order of the day for kings. And the caste system that formed the basis for the Gupta social order permitted a man to marry a woman of equal or lower caste—a dispensation that was not granted to women. Thus, at least when it came to marriage, the emperors seem to have been fairly casual about class distinctions. For example, the Licchavi alliance of which the Guptas were so proud involved such an intercaste marriage, since Chandragupta I, a Brahmin, took as wife a Kshatriya princess, one belonging to the traditional caste of kings and warrior aristocrats.

The luxury enjoyed by courtiers and aristocrats was presumably financed partly by loot from the Gupta conquests, but there were other sources. Samudragupta, pushing into the territory of the forest tribes of India, had enabled an expansion of agriculture. And, under the relaxed but stable administration of Chandragupta II and his immediate successors, commerce flourished. Moreover, there was a lucrative trade with both western Asia and the Roman Empire: Roman gold flowed freely into Gupta lands.

Given such prosperity and the leisure it enabled, great intellects flowered. One scientific genius associated with the Gupta age was mathematician and astronomer Aryabhata, whose work dealt with such abstruse matters as algebraic identities, indeterminate equations, and area and volume. Aryabhata realized that the earth was a sphere, that it rotated on its axis, and that it revolved around the sun. He also knew that lunar eclipses were caused by the earth's shadow falling on the moon. In addition, Aryabhata derived a very accurate value of pi, and in notation he used a decimal system—a method unknown elsewhere in the ancient world, and one whose worth can hardly be exaggerated. But an even more valuable mathematical contribution also dates from Gupta times: numbers themselves, as they are now known. Although their specific author is uncertain, "Arabic" numerals, with their system of nine digits and a zero, are not, in fact, Arabic; they are the product of Indian mathematicians of Gupta times. The notation and decimal systems were adopted by the Arabs—who called mathematics "the Indian science"—and passed along by them to Europe, where it helped form the basis of much invention and discovery.

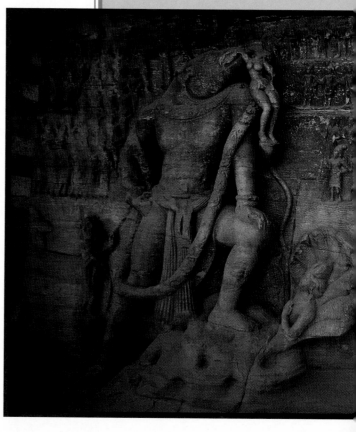

journeys of salvation to the earth in human and animal shapes called avatars. During the first three, he took the shape of a fish, a tortoise, and a boar *(below)*—each one a hero of Indian creation myths. Other incarnations include Rama, the hero of the epic the Ramayana, and Krishna, the widely worshiped deliverer of the sermon of the Bhagavad Gita. Buddha himself was included as the ninth avatar. A 10th—a warrior on horseback or a horse-headed human known as Kalki—is yet to come. When he does, he will cut the thread of time with his sword and bring destruction to the world.

Here Varaha, the boar incarnation of Vishnu, lifts the goddess earth from the churning waters of the "milk-sea ocean," eternity, while crushing the serpent power of the depths beneath his feet. On either side, sages and celestial beings give praise.

The Gupta age was, moreover, a time of great change in religious thought. Buddhism, ascendant since the time of the Mauryas, continued to lose ground to the Hindu practice of bhakti, involving devotion to specific deities. The golden age thus saw the consolidation of the major Brahmanical devotional cults, prominent among them those of Vishnu, Shiva, and the Goddess in her various forms

It was during the classical period that the major Puranas—the mythological, liturgical, and cosmological lore that underpins Hinduism—were compiled, and the two great Indian epics, the Mahabharata and the Ramayana, took on their final form and were accepted both as scripture and as guides in sociopolitical matters. The *Kamasutra*, a sort of how-to manual of erotica, was also written during this era and would be very influential in subsequent Indian art.

Although Brahmanism was waxing and Buddhism waning under the Guptas, all the Hindu sects, as well as Buddhism and Jainism, coexisted peacefully, and there was considerable intermingling and exchange of ideas among them. (In fact, the Buddha himself would be accepted into the Hindu pantheon as one of the avatars of Vishnu.) The amiability was surely due in part to the insistence of the Gupta emperors on religious tolerance: Ardent followers of Vishnu though they were, the Gupta rulers generally had Buddhists among their advisers at court, and they were generous in their patronage of Buddhist monastic centers and universities, such as the one at Nalanda *(pages 138-139)*.

As has always been the case in India, art existed in the service of religion, and the coalescing of the various Hindu devotional cults gave rise to the extensive building of temples and the creation of sculptures to adorn them. Before the time of the Guptas, Indian temples were built of relatively perishable materials, such as timber, brick, and plaster. The golden age, however, saw the rise of stone temples dedicated to Hindu deities, structures made possible mostly through royal and aristocratic patronage.

Hinduism boasts an ancient architectural science called vastu, the first traces of which are set down in the epics and Puranas. The centuries after the Guptas would see the compilation of architectural information in works called vastushastras. This science was probably more theological than technical, however, devised by Brahmins to ensure that the temples fulfilled their primary religious function: to link the world of humans with the world of gods. From a practical point of view, however, the craftsmen who actually built the temples—and produced their marvelous sculptures and paintings—employed their own techniques, unwritten and handed down from generation to generation.

Of northern India's freestanding stone temples built during the golden age, only two are completely preserved, one at Sanchi and one at Tigawa. These are enough, however, to define the essential style of temple building at the time. Their basic architectural schemes involve a square sanctuary connected to a small, pillared porch, both resting on a stone base. The sanctuary's roof consists of horizontal slabs of stone. The stone tower—an architectural feature so distinctive in the great medieval days of Hindu temple building that would follow the Guptas' decline—begins to emerge in the sixth century. A unique ornamental feature that characterizes the Gupta style is the pillar capital, made in the form of pots with foliage. This same feature can be seen in the only cave temples directly associated with Gupta emperors, those carved into the sandstone hills at Udayagiri. More than half of the 20 excavations at this central Indian site consist of rectangular shrine chambers cut into the rock. One shrine has a portico whose columns are adorned with pot and foliage capitals.

A singular legacy that Gupta-age craftsmen would leave for the builders who followed them was the heavily carved, T-shaped temple doorways, featuring amorous couples nestled in lush foliage. The most elaborate of these entranceways can still be seen in the ruins of the Dashavatara temple at Deogarh, in central India, one of only a handful of Gupta temples not completely destroyed by foreign incursions.

Like many sculptors before them, the Gupta artists concentrated their efforts on depicting the human form, whether mortal or divine. In its execution, the most obvious break between the Gupta style and its predecessors came in the treatment of the eyes. Instead of the outward gaze characteristic of the Kushana school, the Buddhas and Jain saints of the Gupta style have downcast eyes, giving the face more-harmonious proportions as well as a distinctly introspective and contemplative character. In the Hindu sculpture of the Guptas there is an increased tendency to give some deities multiple limbs, symbolic of their supernatural powers. Regardless of the number of arms, however, the human forms in Gupta sculpture are more supple and elegant than those of earlier styles, their clothing simpler, and their ornamentation made subservient to the overall unity and visual harmony of the whole.

A line of visitors passes a grand staircase leading up to one of the 11 monasteries that have been uncovered at Nalanda, a center of Buddhist learning until the 12th century. Chinese monks who had made pilgrimages to Nalanda commented on the magnificent temples, including one they said was six stories tall and enclosed an 80-foot-high copper image of Buddha.

The 50-foot-tall temple at Bhitargaon shown below is one of the few brick Hindu temple towers of Gupta times to survive to the present day. The thickness of the walls left space inside for only a 15-foot-square womb chamber in which the gods were worshiped. The tower rising over the chamber symbolized the mythical home of the deities atop the Himalayan peak Kailas.

Clearly, there were great masters among sculptors of the golden age, but they are anonymous: Their culture considered them to be merely the instruments of higher forces, and as such their identities and individual talents were thought unimportant. What mattered was their fitness to translate the divine into concrete forms. To this end, according to ancient literature, they had to undergo ritual purification and to practice prescribed mental disciplines before beginning work. Ironically, despite both their genius and the rigors of their craft, the sculptors and painters of the Gupta age were held in low regard socially.

Of far greater stature among their fellow citizens were writers. And indeed, it is for the brilliance of its Sanskrit literature, more than any other single factor, that the Gupta age is best remembered. This literature had multiple forms, including drama, poetry, court epics, prose romances, and fables. There were many fine writers, including Bhartrihari, whose versatility and verbal gymnastics have caused some scholars to compare him with Rome's Horace. Among the various literary luminaries, however, one man was so preeminent as to occupy a place in Indian letters akin to that of Shakespeare in the West. He was the poet and dramatist Kalidasa, generally believed to have ornamented the court of Chandragupta II.

Three of Kalidasa's plays are known, the most famous being *Shakuntala*, whose plot is drawn from the epic Mahabharata. *Shakuntala* is generally considered the finest play in the Sanskrit language. His best-known poem is called *Cloud Messenger*. Aside from its lyrical genius, the work of Kalidasa offers insight into society under the Guptas. The author seemed especially sensitive to domestic matters—the importance of wives to their

Terra-cotta plaques such as this slightly marred piece decorated the exterior of brick Gupta temples like the one at Bhitargaon. It depicts the two hero bowmen of the Ramayana, *Rama* (left), *an avatar of the god Vishnu, and his brother Lakshmana. The straps across their chests hold arrow quivers on their backs.*

husbands, and the love of Indians for their children. In *Shakuntala*, he writes of wives, "Though they rival the lotus in delicacy, yet surpass the durability of gold in hardships." And of children, he declares that: "With their teeth half-shown in causeless laughter, / and their efforts at talking so sweetly uncertain, / when children ask to sit on his lap / a man is blessed, even by the dirt on their bodies."

Little is known of Kalidasa's personal life. He seems to have been very well versed in Vedic literature, as well as in the religious and secular laws and the sciences of his time.

The cultural grandeur of the golden age is most associated with Chandragupta II, the last of the three great Gupta emperors, who, after ruling some 37 or 38 years, died between AD 413 and 416. The glory of the empire would continue under his son and successor, Kumaragupta I, although it would not be particularly enhanced by him.

Unlike his more forceful predecessors, Kumaragupta was no conqueror. Of the 13 extant inscriptions describing his rule—more than exist for any other Gupta monarch—only one has anything to say about military conquest. Nevertheless, he was evidently an able administrator who smoothly maintained the royal territories that he had inherited; cultural development, peace, and prosperity continued during his 40-year reign. As had his forefathers, Kumaragupta steered the ship of state with a light hand. The central government provided public works and regulated trade, but provinces and districts had considerable leeway in administrative details and local policy making.

One item that did seem to occupy a good deal of Kumaragupta's interest and attention was the minting of coins. Under his generous patronage, mint masters were kept continually busy designing and minting for their monarch, who issued in all no fewer than 13 different types of gold and silver and copper coins—coins showing the king on horseback, the king riding an elephant, the king with bow and arrow, the king with a sword, the king killing lions and tigers and even rhinoceroses. A coin celebrating the Hindu god Kumara, for whom his Gupta namesake apparently had a particular devotion, was also in circulation.

Inscriptions indicate that Skandagupta, who succeeded his father around AD 455, was a man of ability and considerable grit, but it was his misfortune to live in troubled times. From across his northwestern border, the barbaric White Huns came streaming into the empire. Among their early targets for plunder was the city of Mathura, so long a center of great imperial art. It would never recover. Early in his reign, Skandagupta was able to drive the Huns back, but continued onslaughts brought them all the way into central India. Under the strain, the empire began to weaken and crack. Significantly, the coins of Skandagupta tended to be neither as pure as those issued by the great Gupta emperors, nor as finely wrought. There was strife within the Gupta family itself, amounting to contending claims to the throne, possibly because Skandagupta was not born of Kumaragupta's chief queen and was thus not an entirely legitimate successor. Details of the struggle are scant, but the last of the five inscriptions dedicated to Skandagupta is dated AD 466, and it appears that his rule lasted 20 years at most. He had no known sons, and after his tenure the Gupta line, such as it was, continued in the sons of his brother Purugupta.

In the century of confusion following Skandagupta's rule, the empire would fragment into petty kingdoms. There would be seven Gupta kings after Skandagupta, but they would rule over only trivial remnants. In the seventh century there would be a brief revival of the empire—at least of its old territorial extent—and its ruler, a remarkable man, would have at least a tangential connection to the Guptas.

The new king was Harsha, who came from the city of Thanesar, strategically situated in the eastern Punjab at the entrance to the Ganges plain. Harsha's father was a local king who had had some success in fighting off the Huns; his mother was a princess of the later Gupta line. Harsha began his rule in AD 606 when he was only 16 years old after his older brother, Rajyavardhana, was assassinated and his sister, Rajyasri, kidnapped by a rival king. Taking only the modest title of *rajaputra*—prince—Harsha on his ascension went immediately to battle, originally to avenge his siblings. He fought continuously for almost six years, in which time he established his sovereignty over most of northern India. In 612 he had a formal coronation as emperor, setting up his capital at Kanauj (modern Kanyakubja) on the east bank of the Ganges River.

Most of what is known of Harsha comes from two literary sources. Bana, a Sanskrit poet, paid a long visit to Harsha's court and afterward wrote the *Harshacharita*, a romantic account of the king's early days, up until the time Harsha rescued his sister. More informative about the king's later reign is the account of Hsuan Tsang, who, like Fa Hsien in the days of the Guptas, was a Chinese Buddhist monk visiting India. Judging by Hsuan Tsang's account, Harsha as a warrior, savant, and humanitarian rivaled the greatest of his long-dead Gupta ancestors.

The Chinese memoir is not actually needed to affirm Harsha's intellectual prowess. There survive three Sanskrit plays that the emperor himself wrote. As to military matters, however, Hsuan Tsang is most enlightening, reporting that Harsha originally raised a fighting force of 50,000 infantry, 2,000 cavalry, and 5,000 war elephants, and in the six hard years before his coronation "the elephants were not unharnessed nor the soldiers unbelted." After becoming emperor he enlarged his formidable army to include 100,000 cavalry and 60,000 elephants—if Hsuan Tsang did not exaggerate—although, in the main, his fighting days were now over.

In peacetime, the monk observed approvingly, Harsha "practiced to the utmost the rules of temperance, and sought to plant the tree of religious merit to such an extent that he forgot to sleep or to eat. He forbade the slaughter of any living thing or flesh as food throughout the Five Indies on pain of death without pardon."

The four-armed god Shiva is presented whimsically here in the form of the Lord of Ganas, a bejeweled, corpulent dwarf. Ganas are minor deities who serve as Shiva's attendants. The late fifth-century sandstone sculpture was found in central India at Mansar, not far from Nagpur, site of the capital of the Vakatakas.

Hsuan Tsang further credits the king with erecting several thousand Buddhist stupas along the Ganges, and of building throughout his realm hospices staffed with physicians to care for travelers and the poor. In addition, it was the royal practice to travel to Prayag every five years to keep an ancestral custom of distributing his wealth to the poor and to the holy men of various sects. Hsuan Tsang went along to one of these assemblies and described how vassal kings, members of religious orders, and some half a million common people gathered to accept the kingly largesse. Harsha reportedly spent more than two months giving away coins, jewels, clothing, food and drink, flowers, and perfumes.

As in the days of the Guptas, India's various religions got along peacefully under Harsha. The king himself was originally a follower of Shiva, although he later leaned more toward Buddhism. Religion was obviously of great interest to him. In the year 643, while Hsuan Tsang was still at his court, Harsha went to elaborate lengths to arrange an assembly for religious debate. On the Ganges' west bank he built as a site for the event a community of pavilions and rest houses. Along with Harsha and a host of his tributary kings, 4,000 Buddhist monks and 3,000 Brahmins and Jains attended. Hsuan Tsang presented the case for the Mahayana branch of Buddhism, noting later with some smugness that he carried the day. The "followers of error withdrew and disappeared," he wrote.

From Hsuan Tsang's account of his Indian tour, it appears that Harsha had at least some success in reviving the prosperity of the Gupta age. His capital of Kanauj is described as a great center of commerce, and its people were said to lead comfortable and contented lives. As an administrator, the king, harking back not to the Guptas but to the far-off days of Ashoka, traveled constantly to inspect his dominions and hear grievances.

Despite Harsha's tireless work and lavish generosity, however, there were signs of financial strain on his empire: He sometimes substituted grants of land for government salaries, for example, distributing cash payments only in return for military service. Another weakness of his kingdom was that so much of its stability and cohesion relied solely on his own personality and energy. And thus the brief revival of the golden days of the Guptas was not to last. Harsha reigned for a long time—some 42 years—but in the end he fell victim to an assassin. He died without leaving a lawful heir, and his empire quickly disintegrated.

Long before the advent of Harsha—about the time that Skandagupta's ill-fated reign in northern India was drawing to a close—the Vakataka empire to the south was reaching its zenith under the greatest of its emperors, Harishena. Distant from the marauding Huns in the north, Harishena was able to stave off for a time the night that was falling over India with the Gupta decline. Moreover, he was able to give to the golden age before it vanished what was arguably its finest monument: the caves at Ajanta.

Given the evidence of inscriptions, coins, and literary works, it appears that Harishena assumed his dynastic throne in about AD 460 and expanded his empire across southern India from coast to coast. With the Guptas waning, he even pushed forward his northern boundaries to assume some territories that the northern empire had previously held. Of the two dynasties, the Vakatakas were at this time clearly ascendant, and they would remain so for the 17 years of Harishena's kingship.

About two years after Harishena began his rule, work at Ajanta began after a hiatus of some 300 years. Walter M. Spink, an art historian at the University of Michigan at Ann Arbor, has theorized that the labor continued for only about 15 years—a short span that, re-

At Ajanta, a beam of early morning sunlight illuminates the interior of unfinished Cave 24, which was intended to be a monastery. Stonecutters had already cleared out most of the interior and accomplished much smoothing and sculpting of the walls when all work on the cave abruptly stopped following the death of the emperor Harishena in AD 477.

markably, saw the creation of the great murals depicting the glories of the Vakataka court—and then, suddenly, it stopped. The inevitable implication is that this last great flowering of the classical age was willed into existence by Harishena, and it could not survive his death.

Ajanta abounds with inscriptions attesting to the patronage of Harishena's court. It seems that the courtiers, led by chief imperial minister Varahadeva, rushed to contribute to the great Buddhist monument in which their ruler, a Buddhist himself, had taken such an interest. According to Walter Spink, "all the evidence suggests that Ajanta was really inaugurated—made possible—by the combined efforts of a very high-powered and court-connected 'organizing committee,' all of whom for reasons of pride and politics as much as piety probably had a keen interest in being involved from the start."

Yet by AD 480—a few years after Harishena's death—the site was completely abandoned, even though some of the work there was still unfinished. The reason all labor ceased was that there were no longer patrons to finance it: The Vakataka empire, like the Gupta empire before it, was falling apart. As with Harsha, Harishena had himself been the imperial glue that held things together. When he died, the Vakataka realm fell into the hands of his incompetent son, Sarvasena III, who was no match for the forces arrayed against him. A coalition of minor kings mounted an uprising, and in short order the empire collapsed into a jumbled pattern of feudal states.

Thus had two great empires of ancient India appeared, glittered for a time, then guttered out, as though reprising the age-old Hindu notion of the cyclical course of the cosmos, the eternal rise and fall, creation and destruction. But the legacy left by the Guptas and Vakatakas was both lasting and incalculable. Perhaps fitting as their epitaph is an inscription found on one of the magnificent caves of Ajanta: "A man continues to enjoy himself in paradise as long as his memory is green in the world," it says. "One should therefore set up a memorial on the mountains that will endure for as long as the moon and the sun continue."

WHERE GODS AND KINGS MET

In a broad, boulder-strewn valley of southern India stand the sprawling ruins of one of the world's great wonders—Vijayanagara, City of Victory. Yet for all its magnificence, this center of Hindu power and religion is almost unknown outside the Indian subcontinent. Flourishing between the 14th and 16th centuries AD, Vijayanagara so impressed a Persian visitor in 1443 with its "enormous magnitude" and king of "perfect rule" that he declared the city to have no equal. Even today, it is easy to see why he felt that way. Remnants of a massive stone wall, some two and a half miles long and 19 feet high, still run around the city. Formidable gateways like the one shown above lead inside. There, an assemblage of largely deserted buildings—pavilions, temples, and shrines—speaks hauntingly of the grandeur of the past.

Vijayanagara was built and maintained as an ostentatious display of imperial authority in a region of diverse cultures. The city's layout, which included a sacred center as well as a royal zone, reflects the partnership that Hindus believed existed between their kings and their gods. Within the regal precinct still lies the key shrine, which connected the ruler's earthly realm to the spiritual domain of the god Rama, some of whose adventures are supposed to have taken place in the environs. While the outer surface of the building's enclosure wall bears profane images of women, soldiers, horses, and elephants *(used as a background throughout this essay)*, the inner one depicts scenes from the Ramayana, the story of the deity.

In 1565 the City of Victory fell to Muslim invaders, who sacked it and put it to the torch. For more than 400 years it has lain abandoned, with only intermittent efforts on the part of archaeologists to explore and preserve it. Now UNESCO has added Vijayanagara to its World Heritage List of historical sites deserving attention, and concerted efforts are under way to save it from further disintegration.

CENTER OF THE GUIDING SPIRIT

Attempts to draw attention to the neglected riches of Vijayanagara have been aided by the work of Australian photographer John Gollings. His eight years of work there have yielded hundreds of images, from which those used in this essay were selected. Gollings's shot of the Tiruvengalanatha Temple Complex at right serves to underscore the importance of the city's sacred center.

Separated from the royal precinct and urban core by an irrigated valley, this zone consisted not only of grand religious structures, many with large interior courts, such as the one at right, but also of long, colonnaded streets used for processions and markets. Here too existed small tanks, waterworks, and irrigated fields, an indication that food was produced and stored in Vijayanagara's sacred center. The temples directly controlled the management of the fields and their yields, as well as the flow of money and goods in the city.

A ceremonial avenue leads regally to the double-walled temple complex of Tiruvengalanatha, an aspect of Vishnu, in this photograph taken from a nearby slope. The entrance is marked by two monumental gopuras, or gateways. To the right of the complex stretch irrigated lands. Though today's farmers still use some of the city's ancient waterworks, they draw heavily on new systems as well. Their encroachments pose a threat to the ruins.

Viewed from the city's eastern gateway, the towered gopura of the temple of Virupaksha, one of Shiva's names, soars nine stories high in the distance against a backdrop of hills and sky. The temple, the oldest part of which dates from the ninth century, sits today among houses of the village of Hampi. The Tungabhadra River seen winding across the picture was the primary source of irrigation water during ancient times.

Stone wheels on this sculpted copy of a ceremonial chariot in the Vithala Temple once turned on their axles but have now been fixed in place in order to prevent further deterioration. Intended as a shrine for Garuda, the eagle mount of Vishnu, the monument is now missing its brick tower.

Carved from a boulder, this monster-headed figure with bulging eyes depicts Narasimha, a fierce man-lion avatar of Vishnu. Much damaged during the sack of the city, the monolith once included the figure of a goddess, now in pieces on the ground. The 21-foot-tall work has recently been restored.

SEAT OF POWER AND ENLIGHTENMENT

For more than two centuries the royal center of Vijayanagara was the seat of powerful monarchs. Fernao Nuiz, a 16th-century Portuguese visitor, reported that the king maintained an army of 50,000 soldiers, 6,000 of whom were horsemen making up the palace guard. In addition, the monarch had 20,000 shield bearers and spearmen, 3,000 elephant attendants, 1,600 grooms, and 300 horse trainers. Ever on the alert, he employed a small army of spies, and watchtowers *(opposite, far right)* rose high above the walls of the royal enclosure to guard against the approach of enemies.

Domingo Paes, another 16th-century Portuguese traveler, who gained access to the palace, found himself bedazzled by its opulence—a chamber paneled in ivory, another room with a cot suspended from the ceiling on golden chains, an enormous ornamented dance hall. Amid such splendor the king began his daily routine at daybreak with a massage, followed by rigorous exercise and then a bath. After worship, the spiritually and physically refreshed ruler held audience. If, during the course of the day, he grew bored, he could divert himself: He had several wives and 300 to 400 concubines. A further 1,200 women were employed as singers, dancers, and musicians. And outside the royal enclosure, awaiting the king's pleasure, were numerous courtesans famed for their beauty, intelligence, and wealth.

Sides askew, the Madhava Temple dominates the foreground of this view of the royal center. To the right rears an octagonal watchtower. The crumbling walls of the enclosure beyond mark the site where the residence of the king or his commanding general may have stood. Known as the Lotus Mahal, the pavilion in the background with clustered towers may have functioned as a reception hall for the ruler.

The multidomed stable at left once housed the most important of the king's elephants, several to a chamber, with each animal attached to a chain dangling from an iron hook in the ceiling. Abdul Razzaq, the Persian visitor of 1443, commented that the ruler "had a thousand elephants with bodies like mountains and miens like demons." That they were huge is attested by the height of the doorways.

Polished granite columns carved with varied images of Vishnu occupy the inner hall of the Ramachandra Temple. As the most-important religious structure in the middle of the royal center, the temple reminded people that the capital was the city of gods, as well as the realm of kings.

The Square Water Pavilion in the south-east corner of the royal center was probably used by the king and male courtiers for bathing. The steps on the right led down to the pool, where holes in the floor may have been used to brace poles for a shade-making canopy.

A boulder with a shrine in front and a tower on top is situated just outside the Raghunatha Temple. This complex, devoted to Rama, lies in the city's old urban core. Fresh whitewash indicates that the shrine is once again in use as a place of worship. Rama was said to have rested here and to have cleft the rock with his arrows. The large crevice in the foreground serves as a cistern. It is bordered by carved lingas—stylized phalluses emblematic of Shiva—and by Nandi bulls—the mounts of the god.

THE UNIQUE CULTURES OF ANCIENT INDIA

Some 700,000 years ago, hardy bands of Stone Age people were living in the northern Indus Valley and in isolated areas of the Indian subcontinent. By about 7000 BC, some of their descendants settled down at a site called Mehrgarh on a far edge of the Indus Valley. Here they erected a solid mud-brick town and began to domesticate animals and grow cereal crops to feed an expanding population.

Over the course of several millennia, the people of Mehrgarh and other similar settlements developed a civilization that produced such artifacts as the terra-cotta female figurine shown below. And they laid the groundwork for the great urban cultures and empires that would later arise throughout the subcontinent.

HARAPPAN 2600-1800 BC

CARVED STONE SEAL

Named for one of its major urban centers, the Harappan civilization emerged in the broad valley of the Indus River—which would give India its name—in around 2600 BC, and flourished for approximately 800 years. While similar in some respects to the Mesopotamian culture that had arisen to the west, Harappan civilization developed independently and was unique to the subcontinent.

At their great cities of Harappa and Mohenjodaro, the Harappans lived in sturdy brick dwellings served by water supply and drainage systems unmatched anywhere in the ancient world. Hundreds of smaller, equally well-planned towns and villages dotted a vast territory of more than 300,000 square miles.

Harappan merchants carried on a widespread trade, marking their wares with inscribed stone seals such as the one shown above. The script that adorned the seals and other Harappan artifacts has not yet been deciphered, however, leaving many mysteries unsolved.

VEDIC AND EPIC AGES 1800-600 BC

STYLIZED COPPER MAN

By around 1900 BC, Harappan civilization had begun to slip into decline. At about the same time that shifting river courses disrupted agriculture and led to a breakdown in trade networks, a new people, the Indo-Aryans—warlike, seminomadic cattle herders—began spreading out in the northern part of the subcontinent. Soon many of the Harappans' towns were abandoned, although their culture survived in modified form in numerous other settlements scattered throughout the Indus and upper Ganges valleys. During this period of change and uncertainty, inhabitants of the region frequently stashed away mysterious hoards of copper objects such as the figure shown above.

Over time, a new culture arose, based on the language and religion of the Indo-Aryans. Their texts—known as the Vedas—and later epics were the basis for the Hindu religion, which was soon dominated by a priestly class known as Brahmins.

TERRA-COTTA FIGURINE

PRE-MAURYAN AND MAURYAN PERIOD 600-100 BC

LIONS OF ASHOKA

SATAVAHANAS AND KUSHANAS 100 BC-AD 300

KANISHKA COIN

GUPTA EMPIRE AD 300-500

RIVER GODDESS

Dissenting against the authority and elaborate rituals of the Brahmin elite, new faiths began to arise in ancient India. Most influential was Buddhism, founded around 500 BC by the visionary Siddhartha Gautama, which bypassed the need for priests and rituals and offered salvation to all who accepted its simple doctrines and ethics.

Following a brief incursion by the Macedonian conqueror Alexander the Great in 326 BC, a great ruler named Chandragupta Maurya arose and gradually conquered and united all of the small republics and kingdoms that had arisen, thus creating India's first large, centralized empire. His grandson, Ashoka—a convert to Buddhism—dispatched missionaries to numerous parts of Asia and erected throughout his domain large stone pillars inscribed with royal proclamations. One such monument, at Sarnath, was topped with four lions *(above)* that have become the official symbol of the modern Republic of India.

Several decades after the death of Ashoka the long-lived Satavahana dynasty arose in the south, but the northern Mauryan empire splintered into smaller kingdoms that were at the mercy of foreign invaders. From the north came successive waves of Bactrian Greeks, Scythians, Parthians, and finally, the Kushanas, whose realm would eventually stretch from their central Asian homeland to the upper Ganges Valley.

The Kushanas' greatest ruler was Kanishka, whose bearded, spear-bearing figure appears on the coin above. Like Ashoka before him, Kanishka was a Buddhist convert and, by all reports, a benevolent monarch who took a lively interest in his new religion, convening a major conclave to solidify the faith.

Commerce and the arts flourished during his peaceful reign; merchants dealt in goods from China and the Mediterranean world, and sculptors were kept busy embellishing numerous temples and stupas. In time, however, the Kushanas drifted into decline, and by the middle of the third century they had been ousted.

Renowned as the patrons of ancient India's golden age, the Guptas came to power when Chandragupta I, son of a north Indian chieftain, founded the dynasty early in the fourth century. The Guptas expanded their domain through conquest and gained influence over neighboring kingdoms through alliances and wise marriages—most particularly that of Chandragupta II's daughter to a king of the Vakatakas, who ruled over the vast Deccan Plateau.

Under successive Gupta monarchs the empire prospered and the arts and sciences blossomed. Painters, poets, and musicians thrived; artisans crafted graceful works such as the terra-cotta river goddess shown above; a Gupta mathematician devised the all-important decimal system; builders raised Hindu temples whose designs remain the classic Indian architectural form.

But the golden age did not long endure. In the mid fifth century so-called White Huns from central Asia attacked the Guptas, and by the end of the century their empire had been destroyed.

ACKNOWLEDGMENTS

The editors wish to thank the following for their valuable assistance in the preparation of this volume:

K. C. Agrawal, Archaeological Survey of India, Bhopal; David W. Anthony, Hartwick College, Oneonta, N.Y.; Archaeological Survey of India; Alexandra Ardeleanu-Jansen, Forschungsprojekt Mohenjodaro, Rheinisch-Westfalische Technische Hochschule (RWTH), Aachen; Benoy Behl, Bombay; Achille Bianchi, Rome; S. N. Chowdhary, Baroda; Barbara Dales, University of California, Berkeley; John Falconer, British Library, London; Georg Helmes, Forschungsprojekt Mohenjodaro, RWTH, Aachen; Michael Jansen, Forschungsprojekt Mohenjodaro, RWTH, Aachen; Catherine Jarrige, Musée Guimet, Paris; Karl Jettmar, Heidelberg; Pat Kattenhorn, British Library, London; Wibke Lobo, Museum für Indische Kunst SMPK, Berlin; Christian Manhart, UNESCO, Paris; Richard Meadow, Peabody Museum, Cambridge, Mass.; Roberto Meazza, Milan; P. R. Mehendiretta, American Institute of Indian Studies, New Delhi; George Michell, London; Heather Miller, University of Wisconsin, Madison; V. N. Mishra, Deccan College Research Institute, Pune; M. V. Nair, National Research Laboratory for Conservation of Cultural Property, Lucknow; National Museum, New Delhi; Nehru Memorial Museum and Library, New Delhi; Sangitika Nigam, Bombay; Himani Pandey, Indira Gandhi National Center for the Arts, New Delhi; V. S. Parekh, Department of Archaeology and Ancient History, M.S. University of Baroda; Gregory Possehl, University of Pennsylvania Museum, Philadelphia; S. R. Rao, Marine Archaeology Center, National Institute of Oceanography, Goa; Lydia Seager, British Library, London; Kumkum Singh, Archaeological Survey of India, New Delhi; Carla Sinopoli, University of Michigan Museum, Ann Arbor; Franco Sperandei, Rome; Walter Spink; University of Michigan, Ann Arbor; Robert Lindley Vann, University of Maryland, College Park; J. S. Yadav, American Institute of Indian Studies, Varanasi; Marianne Yaldiz, Museum für Indische Kunst SMPK, Berlin.

The quotes from the Rigveda on page 57 are published with the kind permission of the translator, Wendy Doniger (O'Flaherty) from *The Rig Veda*, Penguin Books, 1981.

PICTURE CREDITS

Museum, London. 78: © Lindsay Hebberd/Woodfin Camp & Associates, New York; © Clive Friend, Cobham, England. 79: Bildarchiv Claus Hansmann, Munich/National Museum, New Delhi. 80: Eberhard Thiem, Lotos Film, Kaufbeuren, Germany. 82, 83: Department of Archaeology, M.S. University, Baroda. 84: © The British Library, London; from *The Art and Architecture of India,* by E. Rowland, Yale University Press, 1953—The British Library, London. 85: Roy C. Craven Jr. 86: Archaeological Survey of India. 90, 91: © The British Museum, London. 92: Robert Nickelsberg/Gamma Liaison. 95: © Clive Friend, Cobham, England. 96: Roy C. Craven Jr. 97: © The British Museum, London. 98-100: Prof. Viktor Sarianidi, Institute of Archeology, Russian Academy of Science. 103: Lauros-Giraudon, Paris. 104: © Government Museum, Mathura, India. 105: © Clive Friend, Cobham, England. 106, 107: Akademie der Wissenschaften, Heidelberg. 109: Paolo Koch, Photo Researchers. 110-119: © The British Library, London. 120: Jean-Louis Nou. 122: Hutchison Library, London—art by John Drummond. 123: © Clive Friend, Cobham, England. 124, 125: Benoy K. Behl. 126, 127: © Clive Friend, Cobham, England—National Research Laboratory for Conservation of Cultural Property, Lucknow, India. 128: *5,000 Years of Art of India,* Koninklijke, Smeets Offset B.V., Weert, The Netherlands. 130, 131: Robert Polidori/Planet (2)—© Jay Freis/Image Bank. 132: Courtesy American Institute of Indian Studies, Neg. no. 388.5. 133: The Cleveland Museum of Art, 1994, purchase, from the J. H. Wade Fund, 72.71. 136, 137: Roy C. Craven Jr. 138, 139: Antonio Martinelli. 140: Courtesy American Institute of Indian Studies, Neg. no. A41.78. 141: The Asia Society, New York: Mr. and Mrs. John D. Rockefeller III Collection. 142, 143: Eberhard Thiem, Lotos Film, Kaufbeuren, Germany. 145: Prof. Walter Spink, ACSAA Color Slide Project, Department of the History of Art, University of Michigan. 146-157: John Gollings. 158, 159: Art by Paul Breeden.

BIBLIOGRAPHY

BOOKS

Aditi: The Living Arts of India. Washington, D.C.: Smithsonian Institution Press, 1985.

The Age of God-Kings (Time-Frame series). Alexandria, Va.: Time-Life Books, 1987.

Agrawal, D. P. *The Archaeology of India* (Scandinavian Institute of Asian Studies Monograph Series). London: Curzon Press, 1982.

Agrawala, Prithvi Kumar. *Gupta Temple Architecture.* Varanasi, India: Prithivi Prakashan, 1968.

Allchin, Bridget, and Raymond Allchin. *The Rise of Civilization in India and Pakistan.* Cambridge: Cambridge University Press, 1985.

Allchin, Bridget (ed.). *South Asian Archaeology, 1981.* Cambridge: Cambridge University Press, 1984.

Allchin, F. R., and Norman Hammond (eds.). *The Archaeology of Afghanistan from Earliest Times to the Timurid Period.* London: Academic Press, 1978.

Archer, Mildred. *Early Views of India.* London: Thames and Hudson, 1980.

Archer, Mildred, and Ronald Lightbown. *India Observed.* London: Victoria and Albert Museum, 1982.

Asher, Frederick M. *The Art of Eastern India, 300-800.* Minneapolis: University of Minnesota Press, 1980.

Bakker, Hans. *Ayodhya* (Part 1). Groningen, The Netherlands: Egbert Forsten, 1986.

Bandaranayake, Senake. "Sigiriya." In *The Cultural Triangle of Sri Lanka.* Paris: UNESCO/CCF, 1993.

Banerjee, Manabendu. *Historical and Social Interpretations of the Gupta Inscriptions.* Calcutta: Sanskrit Pustak Bhandar, 1989.

Barbarian Tides (Time-Frame series). Alexandria, Va.: Time-Life Books, 1987.

Basham, A. L. *The Wonder that Was India.* New York: Macmillan, 1959.

Bayly, C. A. (ed.). *The Raj.* London: National Portrait Gallery, 1990.

Bechert, Heinz (ed.). *The Dating of the Historical Buddha.* Göttingen: Vandenhoeck and Ruprechtin, 1991.

Bechert, Heinz, and Richard Gombrich (eds.). *The World of Buddhism.* London: Thames and Hudson, 1984.

Begley, Vimala, and Richard Daniel De Puma (eds.). *Rome and India.* Madison: University of Wisconsin Press, 1991.

Bhatia, O. P. Singh. *The Imperial Guptas.* Delhi: Surjeet Book Depot, 1962.

Blurton, T. Richard. *Hindu Art.* Cambridge: Harvard University Press, 1993.

Bongard-Levin, G. M. *Mauryan India.* New Delhi: Sterling, 1985.

Bruhn, Thomas P. *A Journey to Hindoostan.* Storrs, Conn.: William Benton Museum of Art, University of Connecticut, 1987.

Chakrabarti, Dilip K.:
The External Trade of the Indus Civilization. New Delhi: Munshiram Manoharlal, 1990.
Theoretical Issues in Indian Archaeology. New Delhi: Munshiram Manoharlal, 1988.

Chakrabarti, Hiren (ed.). *European Artists and India, 1700-1900.* Calcutta: Trustees of the Victoria Memorial, 1987.

Chandra, Pramod. *The Sculpture of India, 3000 B.C.-1300 A.D.* Washington, D.C.: Board of Trustees, National Gallery of Art, 1985.

Chhabra, B. Ch., et al. (eds.). *Reappraising Gupta History for S. R. Goyal.* New Delhi: Aditya Prakashan, 1992.

Les Cités Oubliées de l'Indus. Paris: Association Française d'Action Artistique Paris, 1988.

Clarke, Peter B. *The World's Religions.* Pleasantville, N.Y.: Reader's Digest

Association, 1993.

Craven, Roy C. *Indian Art*. London: Thames and Hudson, 1986.

Crowther, Margaret, and Elizabeth Pichon (eds.). *The World Atlas of Archaeology*. London: Mitchell Beazley, 1985.

Dani, A. H. *Recent Archaeological Discoveries in Pakistan*. Paris: UNESCO, 1988.

Dani, A. H., and V. M. Masson (eds.). *History of Civilizations of Central Asia* (Vol. 1). Paris: UNESCO, 1992.

Dehejia, Vidya. *Early Buddhist Rock Temples: A Chronology*. London: Thames and Hudson, 1972.

Desai, Vishakha N., and Darielle Mason. *Gods, Guardians, and Lovers*. New York: Asia Society Galleries, 1993.

Doshi, Saryu (ed.):
India and Greece. Bombay: Marg Publications, 1985.
Maharashtra. Bombay: Marg Publications, 1985.

Ehrich, Robert W. (ed.). *Chronologies in Old World Archaeology* (Vol. 1). Chicago: University of Chicago Press, 1992.

The Encyclopedia Americana International Edition (Vol. 16). Danbury: Grolier, 1986.

Eliade, Mircea. *Yoga* (2nd ed.). Translated by Willard R. Trask. Princeton: Princeton University Press, 1969.

Erdosy, George. *Urbanisation in Early Historic India*. Oxford: B.A.R., 1988.

Fairservis, Walter A., Jr. *The Roots of Ancient India*. Chicago: University of Chicago Press, 1975.

Finegan, Jack. *An Archaeological History of Religions of Indian Asia*. New York: Paragon House, 1989.

Fritz, John M., and George Michell. *City of Victory: Vijayanagara*. New York: Aperture Foundation, 1991.

Godrej, Pheroza, and Pauline Rohatgi. *Scenic Splendours*. London: British Library, 1989.

Gray, Basil (ed.). *The Arts of India*. Oxford: Phaidon Press, 1981.

Grover, Satish. *The Architecture of India*. New Delhi: Vikas Publishing House, 1980.

Gupta, S. P. (ed.). *Kushana Sculptures from Sanghol (1st-2nd Century A.D.)*, Vol. 1. New Delhi: National Museum, 1985.

Gupte, Ramesh Shankar, and B. D. Mahajan. *Ajanta, Ellora and Au-rangabad Caves*. Bombay: D. B. Taraporevala, 1962.

Halliday, Tony (ed.). *Pakistan*. Hong Kong: APA Publications, 1990.

Hamblin, Dora Jane, and the Editors of Time-Life Books. *The First Cities* (The Emergence of Man series). New York: Time-Life Books, 1973.

Harle, J. C.:
The Art and Architecture of the Indian Subcontinent. Harmondsworth, U.K.: Penguin Books, 1986.
Gupta Sculpture. Oxford: Clarendon Press, 1974.

Harpur, James (ed.). *The World's Religions*. Pleasantville, N.Y.: Reader's Digest Association, 1993.

Hawkes, Jacquetta:
The First Great Civilizations. New York: Alfred A. Knopf, 1973.
Mortimer Wheeler. London: Weidenfeld and Nicolson, 1982.

Hawkes, Jacquetta (ed.). *Atlas of Ancient Archaeology*. New York: McGraw-Hill, 1974.

Hughes, James (ed.). *The World Atlas of Archaeology*. London: dilithium Press, 1988; distributed in U.S. by Crown Publishers.

Huntington, Susan L. *The Art of Ancient India*. New York: Weatherhill, 1985.

India: Fairs & Festivals. Tokyo: Morihiro Oki, 1989.

Ingpen, Robert, and Philip Wilkinson. *Encyclopedia of Mysterious Places*. New York: Viking Studio Books, 1990.

Inside India (rev. ed.). New Delhi: Himalayan Books, 1988.

Ions, Veronica. *Indian Mythology* (Library of the World's Myths and Legends series). New York: Peter Bedrick Books, 1987.

Israel, Samuel, and Bikram Grewal (eds.). *India*. Hong Kong: APA Publications, 1993.

Jacobson, Doranne. *India: Land of Dreams and Fantasy*. New York: Todtri Productions, 1992.

Jansen, Michael:
Die Indus-Zivilisation. Cologne: DuMont Buchverlag, 1986.
Mohenjo-Daro. Bergisch Gladbach, Germany: Frontinus-Gesellschaft, 1993.

Jansen, Michael, Máire Mulloy, and Günter Urban (eds.). *Forgotten Cities on the Indus*. Mainz: Verlag Philipp von Zabern, 1987.

Jarrige, Jean-François, and Marielle Santoni. *Fouilles De Pirak* (Vol. 1). Paris: Diffusion de Boccard, 1979.

Jettmar, Karl. *Between Gandhāra and the Silk Roads*. Islamabad: Lok Virsa Institute, 1991.

Keay, John. *India Discovered*. London: Collins, 1988.

Kenoyer, Jonathan Mark. "Interaction Systems, Specialized Crafts and Culture Change: The Indus Valley Tradition and the Indo-Gangetic Tradition in South Asia." In *Language, Material Culture, and Ethnicity*, edited by George Erdosy. Berlin: Mouton, DeGruyter, in press.

Kenoyer, Jonathan M., and Heather M.-L. Miller. "Metal Technologies of the Indus Valley Tradition in Pakistan and Western India." In *Archaemetallurgy of the Asian Old World*, Monograph Series No. 89, edited by Vince C. Pigott. Philadelphia: University Museum, in press.

Khandalavala, Karl (ed.). *The Golden Age*. Bombay: Marg Publications, 1991.

Khanna, Amar Nath. *Archaeology of India*. New Delhi: Clarion, 1981.

Knox, Robert. *Amaravati*. London: British Museum Press, 1992.

Kumar, Brajmohan. *Archaeology of Pataliputra and Nalanda*. Delhi: Ramanand Vidya Bhawan, 1987.

Lal, Makkhan. *Settlement History and Rise of Civilization in Ganga-Yamuna Doab (from 1500 B.C. to 300 A.D)*. Delhi: B. R. Publishing, 1984.

Lal, B. B. and S. P. Gupta (eds.). *Frontiers of the Indus Civilization*. New Delhi: Books & Books, 1984.

Legrain, L. *Ur Excavations: Seal Cylinders* (Vol. 10). London: The British Museum and the University Museum, University of Pennsylvania, 1951.

Lerner, Martin. *The Flame and the Lotus*. New York: The Metropolitan Museum of Art, 1984.

Longhurst, A. H. *Hampi Ruins*. New Delhi: Asian Educational Services, 1987.

Majumdar, R. C. (ed.). *The Classical Age (The History and Culture of the Indian People)*. Bombay: Bharatiya Vidya Bhavan, 1962.

Mallory, J. P. *In Search of the Indo-Europeans*. London: Thames and Hudson, 1989.

Marshall, John (ed.). *Mohenjo-Daro*

and the Indus Civilization. London: Arthur Probsthain, 1931.

Mathur, Asharani (ed.).:
India. New Delhi: Festival of India, Brijbasi Printers, 1987.
The Great Tradition. New Delhi: Festival of India, Brijbasi Printers, 1988.

Meadow, Richard H. (ed.). *Harappa Excavations, 1986-1990*. Madison, Wis.: Prehistory Press, 1991.

Mehta, R. N., and S. N. Chowdhary. *Excavation at Devnimori*. Baroda, India: University of Baroda, 1966.

Michell, George:
The Hindu Temple. New York: Harper & Row, 1977.
The Penguin Guide to the Monuments of India (Vol. 1). London: Viking, 1989.
The Vijayanagara Courtly Style. New Delhi: Manohar Publications, 1992.

Michell, George (ed.). *In the Image of Man*. London: Weidenfeld and Nicolson, 1982.

Miller, Barbara Stoler (ed.). *The Powers of Art*. Delhi: Oxford University Press, 1992.

Misra, V. N., and Peter Bellwood. *Recent Advances in Indo-Pacific Prehistory*. New Delhi: Oxford & IBH, 1985.

Mitra, Debala. *Buddhist Monuments*. Calcutta: Sahitya Samsad, 1971.

Mitter, Partha. *Much Maligned Monsters*. Oxford: Clarendon Press, 1977.

Mookerjee, Ajit. *Ritual Art of India*. London: Thames and Hudson, 1985.

Mukherjee, Chhanda. *Gupta Numismatic Art*. Delhi: Agam Kala Prakashan, 1991.

Norman, Bruce. *Footsteps*. Topsfield, Mass.: Salem House, 1988.

O'Flaherty, Wendy Doniger (ed.). *Elephanta*. Princeton: Princeton University Press, 1983.

O'Flaherty, Wendy Doniger (transl.). *The Rig Veda*. London: Penguin Books, 1981.

Olender, Maurice. *The Languages of Paradise: Race, Religion, and Philology in the Nineteenth Century*. Translated by Arthur Goldhammer. Cambridge: Harvard University Press, 1992.

Pal, Pratapaditya:
The Ideal Image. New York: Asia Society, 1978.
Indian Sculpture, circa 500 B.C.-

A.D. 700 (Vol. 1). Los Angeles: Los Angeles County Museum of Art and University of California Press, 1986.
The Sensuous Immortals. Los Angeles: Los Angeles County Museum of Art, 1977.

Pal, Pratapaditya, and Vidya Dehejia. *From Merchants to Emperors*. Ithaca: Cornell University Press, 1986.

Pandey, C. B. *Mauryan Art*. Delhi: Bharatiya Vidya Prakashan, 1982.

Parpola, Asko. "Bangles, Sacred Trees and Fertility Interpretations of the Indus Script Relating to the Cult of Skanda-Kumāra." In *South Asian Archaeology, 1987,* edited by Maurizio Taddei. Rome: Istituto Italiano per il Medio ed Estremo Oriente, 1990.

Possehl, Gregory L. *Kulli*. Durham, N.C.: Carolina Academic Press, 1986.

Possehl, Gregory L. (ed.):
Ancient Cities of the Indus. New Delhi: Vikas Publishing House, 1979.
Harappan Civilization. New Delhi: Oxford & IBH, 1982.
Harappan Civilization (2nd rev. ed.). New Delhi: Oxford & IBH, 1993.

Poster, Amy G. *From Indian Earth*. New York: The Brooklyn Museum, 1986.

Prasad, Kameshwar. *Cities, Crafts and Commerce under the Kusanas*. Delhi: Agam Kala Prakashan, 1984.

Radhakrishnan, Sarvepalli, and Charles A. Moore (eds.). *A Source Book in Indian Philosophy*. Princeton: Princeton University Press, 1957.

Rajasekhara, Sindigi. *Masterpieces of Vijayanagara Art*. Bombay: Taraporevala, 1983.

Rao, M. S. Nagaraja. *Vijayanagara*. Mysore, India: Directorate of Archaeology and Museums, Government of Karnataka, 1988.

Rao, S. R. *Lothal and the Indus Civilization*. New York: Asia Publishing House, 1973.

Ratnagar, Shereen. *Encounters*. Delhi: Oxford University Press, 1981.

Renfrew, Colin. *Archaeology and Language*. New York: Cambridge University Press, 1987.

Rohatgi, Pauline, and Pheroza Godrej (eds.). *India: A Pageant of Prints*. Bombay: Marg Publications, 1989.

Ross, Nancy Wilson. *Three Ways of Asian Wisdom*. New York: Simon and Schuster, 1966.

Roy, T. N. *The Ganges Civilization*. New Delhi: Ramanand Vidya Bhawan, 1983.

Sankalia, Hasmukh Dhirajlal, Shantaram Bhalchandra Deo, and Zainuddin Dawood Ansari. *Chalcolithic Navdatoli: The Excavations at Navdatoli, 1957-59*. Poona: The Deccan College Postgraduate and Research Institute; Baroda: The Maharaja Sayajirao University, 1971.

Sarianidi, Victor. *The Golden Hoard of Bactria*. New York: Harry N. Abrams, 1985.

Sastri, Hiranand. *Nalanda and Its Epigraphic Material (Asian Arts and Archaeology Series No. 3)*. Delhi: Sri Satguru Publications, 1986.

Schulberg, Lucille, and the Editors of Time-Life Books. *Historic India* (Great Ages of Man series). New York: Time-Life Books, 1968.

Schwartzberg, Joseph E. (ed.). *A Historical Atlas of South Asia (rev. ed.)*. New York: Oxford University Press, 1992.

Shaffer, Jim G. "The Indo-Aryan Invasions: Cultural Myth and Archaeological Reality." In *The People of South Asia,* edited by John R. Lukacs. New York: Plenum Press, 1984.

Shaikh, Khurshid Hasan, and Syed M. Ashfaque. *Moenjodaro: A 5,000-Year-Old Legacy*. Paris: UNESCO, 1981.

Sharma, G. R. *Memoirs of the Archaeological Survey of India*. Delhi: Archaeological Survey of India, Government of India, 1969.

Shearer, Alistair. *The Traveler's Key to Northern India*. New York: Alfred A. Knopf, 1983.

Singh, Raghubir. *Ganga*. Hong Kong: Perennial Press, 1974.

Smith, Bardwell L. (ed.). *Essays on Gupta Culture*. Delhi: Motilal Banarsidass, 1983.

Smith, H. Daniel (ed.). *Selections from Vedic Hymns*. Berkeley: McCutchan, 1968.

Smith, Vincent A. *Asoka*. Delhi: S. Chand, 1964.

Spink, Walter M. *Ajanta*. Ann Arbor: Asian Art Archives of the University of Michigan, 1994.

Srinivasan, Doris Meth (ed.). *Mathura*. New Delhi: American Institute of Indian Studies, 1989.

Srinivasan, Radhika. *Cultures of the World: India.* New York: Marshall Cavendish, 1990.

Stein, Burton. *The New Cambridge History of India.* Cambridge: Cambridge University Press, 1989.

Stutley, Margaret. *The Illustrated Dictionary of Hindu Iconography.* London: Routledge & Kegan Paul, 1985.

Taddei, Maurizio. *Monuments of Civilization.* London: Cassell, 1977.

Taddei, Maurizio (ed.). "South Asian Archaeology, 1987." Proceedings of the Ninth International Conference of the Association of South Asian Archaeologists in Western Europe. Rome: Istituto Italiano per il Medio ed Estremo Oriente, 1990.

Thapar, B. K. *Recent Archaeological Discoveries in India.* Paris: UNESCO, 1985.

Thapar, Romila. *From Lineage to State.* Bombay: Oxford University Press, 1984.

Vats, Madho Sarup. *Excavations at Harappā.* Delhi: Manager of Publications, 1940.

Vergessene Städte Am Indus. Mainz: Verlag Philipp von Zabern, 1987.

Vidale, Massimo. "Specialized Producers and Urban Elites." In *Old Problems and New Perspectives in the Archaeology of South Asia*, edited by J. M. Kenoyer, Wisconsin Archaeological Reports, Vol. 2. Madison: University of Wisconsin, 1989.

Watson, Francis. *A Concise History of India.* New York: Scribners, 1975.

Wheeler, Mortimer:
  Civilizations of the Indus Valley and Beyond. London: Thames and Hudson, 1966.
  Early India and Pakistan to Ashoka (Ancient Peoples and Places series). New York: Frederick A. Praeger, 1959.
  The Indus Civilization. Cambridge: Cambridge University Press, 1968.

Williams, Joanna Gottfried. *The Art of Gupta India.* Princeton: Princeton University Press, 1982.

Wolpert, Stanley. *India.* Berkeley: University of California Press, 1991.

Wosien, Maria-Gabriele. *Sacred Dance.* New York: Thames and Hudson, 1986.

Zaheer, Mohammad. *The Temple of Bhītārgaon.* Delhi: Agam Kala Prakashan, 1981.

Zimmer, Heinrich. *The Art of Indian Asia* (Vol. 1). Princeton: Princeton University Press, 1960.

PERIODICALS

Agrawal, D. P., et al. "Study of Biodeterioration of the Ajanta Wall Paintings." *International Biodeterioration*, Vol. 24, 1988.

Edwards, Mike W. "An Eye for an Eye: Pakistan's Wild Frontier." *National Geographic*, January 1977.

Erdösy, G. "Early Historic Cities of Northern India." *South Asian Studies*, Vol. 3, 1987.

Fairservis, Walter A., Jr. "The Script of the Indus Valley Civilization." *Scientific American*, March 1983.

Fritz, John M., and George Michell. "Interpreting the Plan of a Medieval Hindu Capital, Vijayanagara." *World Archaeology*, June 1987.

Fritz, John M., George Michell, and M. S. Nagaraja Rao. "Vijayanagara: The City of Victory." *Archaeology*, March/April 1986.

Gray, Harold Farnsworth. "Sewerage in Ancient and Mediaeval Times." *Sewage Works Journal*, September 1940.

Halim, M. A. "Kilns, Bangles and Coated Vessels." *Interim Reports*, edited by M. Jansen and G. Urban, 1984.

Jaffrey, Madhur. "After Centuries of Neglect, India Is Restoring the Eerily Lovely Painted Caves of Ajanta." *Smithsonian*, August 1976.

Jarrige, Jean-François, and Richard H. Meadow. "The Antecedents of Civilization in the Indus Valley." *Scientific American*, August 1980.

Kenoyer, Jonathan M.:
  "The Indus Civilization: Unfathomed Depths of South Asian Culture." *Wisconsin Academy Review*, March 1987.
  "The Indus Valley Tradition of Pakistan and Western India." *Journal of World Prehistory*, Vol. 5, No. 4, 1991.
  "Ornament Styles of the Indus Valley Tradition" *Paléorient*, Vol. 17/2, 1991.
  "Shell Working Industries of the Indus Civilization: A Summary." *Paléorient*, Vol. 10/1, 1984.

Lal, B. B.:
  "Excavation at Hastināpura and Other Explorations in the Upper Ganga and Sutlej Basins, 1950-52."
  Ancient India: Bulletin of the Archaeological Survey of India, Nos. 10 and 11, 1954 and 1955.
  "The Two Indian Epics vis-à-vis Archaeology." *Antiquity*, Vol. 55, 1981.

Lal, Makkhan: "Iron Tools, Forest Clearance and Urbanisation in the Gangetic Plains." *Man and Environment*, Vol. 10, 1986.

Malik, Amita. "Ajanta: From Darkness into Light." *Hindustan Times*, Feb. 2, 1992.

Mallick, Veena. "A Magnificent Obsession." *Metropolis*, April 17, 1993.

Mughal, M. Rafique:
  "Further Evidence of the Early Harappan Culture in the Greater Indus Valley." *South Asian Studies*, Vol. 6, 1990.
  "New Evidence of the Early Harappan Culture from Jalilpur, Pakistan." *Archaeology*, April 1974.

Parpola, Asko. "The Indus Script: A Challenging Puzzle." *World Archaeology*, Vol. 17, no. 3, 1986.

Pope, Gregory T. "Horsepower, 2000 B.C." *Popular Mechanics*, May 1994.

Ray, Himanshu P. "Early Buddhist Caves of the Western Deccan." *Expedition*, Vol. 30, no. 2, 1988.

Shahani, Roshan. "In a New Light." *Sunday Times of India*, April 25, 1993.

Spink, Walter M. "The Caves at Ajanta." *Archaeology*, November/December 1992.

Vann, Robert Lindley:
  "Monasteries, Gardens, and Palaces of Ancient Sri Lanka." *Asian Art*, Vol. 6, no. 3, Summer 1993.
  "The Palace and Gardens of Kasayapa at Sigiriya, Sri Lanka." *Archaeology*, July/August 1987.

Weintraub, Boris. "Striking New Images of Cave Paintings in India." *National Geographic*, November 1993.

Wilford, John Noble. "Remaking the Wheel: Evolution of the Chariot." *New York Times*, Feb. 22, 1994.

OTHER SOURCES

Anthony, David W., and Nikolai B. Vinogradov. "Bronze Age Chariot Burials in the Ural Steppes." Unpublished report, November 1993.

Gail, Adalbert J., and Gerd J. R. Mevissen (eds.). "South Asian Archaeology, 1991." In "Eleventh International Conference of the Association of

South Asian Archaeologists in Western Europe." Conference proceedings. Stuttgart, 1993.

Kenoyer, Jonathan Mark: "Experimental Studies of Indus Valley Technology at Harappa." Preliminary draft. Paper presented at the 12th International Conference of the Association of South Asian Archaeologists in Western Europe, Helsinki, July 1-7, 1993.
Telephone interview on bangles, June 9, 1994.

Kenoyer, Jonathan Mark (ed.) "Old Problems and New Perspectives in the Archaeology of South Asia." *Wisconsin Archaeological Reports,* Vol. 2, 1989.

Khan, F. A. "Preliminary Report on Kot Diji Excavations, 1957-58." Pakistan Department of Archaeology.

Meadow, Richard H., and Jonathan Mark Kenoyer. "Harappa Archaeological Research Project." Report submitted to the Director General of Archaeology and Museums, Govern-

ment of Pakistan, Nov. 1, 1993.

Spink, Walter M. "Making Ajanta." In "Proceedings of the South Asia Seminar." Philadelphia: Department of South Asia Regional Studies, 1988.

Spodek, Howard, and Doris Meth Srinivasan (eds.). "Urban Form and Meaning in South Asia: The Shaping of Cities from Prehistoric to Precolonial Times." Center for the Advanced Study in the Visual Arts. Symposium Papers 15. Washington, D.C.: National Gallery of Art, 1993.

INDEX

N

MESOPOTAMIA

TILLYA TEPE
APHRODITE

PERSIAN GULF

BALUCHISTA

OMAN

ARABI

RED SEA

MOHENJODARO BOAT SEAL

INDIA